Help Heavenward

Help Heavenward

Guidance and Strength for the Christian's Life-Journey

Octavius Winslow

'Lord, help me' (*Matt.* 15:25)

THE BANNER OF TRUTH TRUST

THE BANNER OF TRUTH TRUST
3 Murrayfield Road, Edinburgh EH12 6EL, UK
P O Box 621, Carlisle, PA 17013, U S A

*

First published by James Nisbet 1869
First Banner of Truth Edition 2000
ISBN 0 85151 775 7

*

Typeset in Zapf Calligraphic by
Gardner Graphics, Grand Rapids,
Michigan, USA

Printed in Great Britain
by Bell & Bain Ltd., Glasgow

FOREWORD

We are deeply grateful to the Banner of Truth Trust for this reprint of Octavius Winslow's treasured volume *Help Heavenward*. As is true of all of Winslow's writings, this volume is replete with memorable statements and written for spiritual edification.

This book provides invaluable help to Christians on their way to heaven. Chapter 1 presents the Christian as someone on the way home to heaven. Chapter 2 deals with the critical, yet sorely neglected, theme of progressive sanctification, steering between denial and exaggeration of that process. Winslow focuses in chapter 3 on 'the gentleness of Christ', showing how Christ leads burdened believers onward and calls them to imitate that spirit. Every cloud in the believer's life is Christ's chariot to lead him to glory, chapter 4 teaches. Chapter 5 shows that trials promote spiritual instruction, prayer, spirituality, moral purity – all of which prepare the Christian for heaven. Chapter 6 shows that as the believer progresses to his eternal home, Christ loosens his bonds, delivering him from the world and Satan, providing him with the Spirit's seal of adoption, and working evangelical obedience in him.

Chapter 7 shows how the believer transfers all his cares to God, including mental anxiety, depression, and difficulty in discerning God's will. In the next chapter Winslow explains how self-examination, when properly undertaken, can aid us in our journey to heaven. In chapter 9 he urges God's children to repent of all backsliding, and in chapter 10 he provides directions on how to face death. The book concludes by ushering the believer into his Father's house.

Help Heavenward, a practical handbook on sanctification with heaven ever in view, is devotional writing at its finest. I know of no better book to give to Christians as they struggle in this sinful world to live in obedience to their Saviour. Use this book to become acquainted with those sacred truths of Scripture that the Spirit uses to mould our thoughts, words, and actions for Christlike living.

Octavius Winslow (1808-1878) was descended from Edward Winslow, a Pilgrim Father who braved the Atlantic to go to the New World on the Mayflower in 1620. Octavius's father, Thomas, an army captain stationed in London, died when he was seven years old. Shortly after that, his God-fearing mother took her family of ten children to New York. All of the children became Christians, and three sons became ministers. Octavius later wrote a book about his family's experiences from his mother's perspective, titled *Life in Jesus: A Memoir of Mrs. Mary Winslow, Arranged from her Correspondence, Diary and Thoughts.*

Winslow was ordained as a minister in 1833 in New York. He later moved to England where he became one of the most valued Nonconformist ministers of the nineteenth century, largely due to the earnestness of his preaching and the excellence of his prolific writings. He held pastorates in Leamington Spa, Bath, and Brighton. He was also a popular speaker for special occasions, such as the opening of C. H. Spurgeon's Metropolitan Tabernacle in 1861.

Winslow wrote more than forty books, most of

which went through several printings. His Reformed convictions were clearly indicated in titles such as *Born Again, or, from Grace to Glory; Heaven Opened; The Fulness of Christ; Christ Ever with You; The Glory of the Redeemer in His Person and Work; The Man of God, or, Spiritual Religion Explained and Enforced; The Tree of Life; Emmanuel, or the Titles of Christ; Hidden Life; Midnight Harmonies; Morning Thoughts; Evening Thoughts; Divine Realities; No Condemnation in Christ Jesus; Grace and Truth; Human Sympathy; The Inquirer Directed to an Experimental and Practical View of the Atonement; The Inquirer Directed to an Experimental and Practical View of the Work of the Holy Spirit; Personal Declension and Revival of Religion in the Soul; The Silver Trumpet; Christ the Theme of the Missionary; Glimpses of the Truth as it is in Jesus.*

Winslow was not bound to any denomination, but he did cling to old Puritan theology. In books such as *Help Heavenward*, he promoted an experimental knowledge of the precious truths of God, such as our corrupt nature, and Jesus Christ crucified for sinners, resulting in a life of gratitude. After a short illness, Octavius Winslow died on March 5, 1878, and was buried in Abbey Cemetery, Bath.

We trust this book will be helpful to many. It offers preaching to the preacher before he preaches to others. It offers theology that engages the heart as it transforms the will. And it offers material to help every believer fight the good fight of faith on the way to glory. May God bless this book to people today as it blessed those who read it in Winslow's day.

— Dr. Joel R. Beeke

Puritan Reformed Theological Seminary
Grand Rapids, Michigan

CONTENTS

AUTHOR'S PREFACE

It is one, and not the least impressive, of the many wise and condescending arrangements of God, that by human agency his Church should be gathered, succoured, and guided to its destined glory. Any other than an instrumentality that should engirdle its object with a sympathy entwining itself with all the circumstances of the Christian life, would fail of meeting the case. How could *angels* assist us heavenward? Invisible and noiseless, they undoubtedly encircle our path, performing some high behest of God in the government of his Church; beyond this, how shadowy their existence, and how incompetent their aid! But let us deal with *man*. Let *him* address us in grief to whom sorrow is not a strange thing. Let him chide our infirmities who himself is a partaker of human weakness. Let him succour us in temptation who has himself been wounded by the archers. Let him instruct and lead us whose feet have travelled the path we tread, and we are truly and effectually helped. Such an agency God employs. This fact it is which so inexpressibly endears Christ, the true Helper, to his people, as peerless among his fellows, as a brother pre-eminent among his brethren. While he is wakeful to all their circumstances *as man,* he is prepared to succour them from his infinite resources *as God.*

It is this view of human agency in the history of the Church of Christ which has emboldened the author to write, and having written, to offer to the Christian public, the present volume. It is not all that he desired, or even designed it should be. He has failed to introduce many important topics, from his anxiety to restrict himself within the limits of a portable volume, and from allowing the subjects he has discussed to grow beneath his hand. He trusts, however, that those which the book contains will, with the divine blessing, meet a few of the more important and urgent cases in the Church of Christ in which a little timely help is needed and will be most welcome. The path to heaven is thronged with impediments, and the soul of Zion's traveller is often much discouraged by reason of the way. If this lowly proffer of aid in a journey the most difficult and momentous that human foot ever trod – the soul's travel to a blissful eternity – but guides the hesitating or confirms the faltering step of a solitary Christian pilgrim; if it brings a single soul closer to Christ, and enthrones him more simply and supremely upon the believing, loving, clinging heart; if it but quell a fear, remove a doubt, loosen a bond, shed a gleam upon the dreary way, the effort will not be without an adequate result, nor God without some degree of glory.

Nor let any reader of this volume suppose that nothing is really gained in his Christian journey by a *single step* heavenward. Many sincere Christians deem that they make no progress in the divine life because they do not compass all that they desire. But this should not be. An artist may not perfectly imitate his model, nor a marksman pierce the centre, but does it follow that there has been in the attempt no triumph of genius and of skill? One real view of Jesus, one corruption subdued, one temptation vanquished, one worldly fetter broken, one sunbeam of holy joy shining upon the soul, is a moral victory achieved, a spiritual blessing possessed, more momentous than the taking of a city, and more enriching than the conquest of a world. It may be through deep trial, in the face of powerful opposition and beset by great weakness, that that advanced step has been made; nevertheless it has brought the heart nearer to God, has transcribed some lineament of Jesus to the soul, and is so much actual gain in the believer's progress towards, and in his meetness for, heaven.

And for this little help afforded, the author ventures to ask for himself personally a large boon in return – *the help of the reader's prayers!* Greatly does he need them, that his own soul may prosper and be in health. It is a solemn, a fearful thing to be a mere fingerpost heavenward – advancing others, stationary ourselves! Ministers of the gospel and Christian writers are in great peril of this. Oh that there were more especial and earnest prayer on the part of the church for her spiritual instructors and guides! It is assuming too much to suppose, and it argues a lamentable ignorance of the power of habit in those who suppose it, that constant contact with the things of eternity – the professional studies and employments of the Christian minister – are necessarily promotive of personal piety. Alas, it is too frequently the reverse! May we not by our very familiarity with spiritual things, in consequence of the innate sinfulness of our nature, come to lose much of the holy and vivid impression and power of their spirituality and beauty? And while other souls beneath our unwearied culture are beautified and enriched with all the fruit and flower of holiness, rejoicing and blossoming as the rose, our own presents to the eye the sad spectacle of dreariness, sterility, and neglect! 'They made me the keeper of the vineyards; but mine own vineyard have I not kept' (*Song of Sol.* 1:6). Sincerely and earnestly, then, does the author bespeak for himself, as for his brethren, the spiritual intercessions of the Church of God, for increased personal grace, holiness, and love: 'Ye also helping together by prayer for us' (*2 Cor.* 1:11). It is by this mutual help, this reciprocated obligation, God increases our individual stores of spiritual blessing. The church, while moulding by its prayers a holy, spiritual, vigorous ministry, is at the same moment immensely augmenting her own sources of wealth and power. The earth which contributes its moisture, and the shaded spring its vapour, to freight and enrich the clouds that sail in azure light and glory above us, receives in return from those clouds the quickening dew and the fertilizing shower which replenish the fountains and mantle all nature with verdure, perfume, and fruit. The moral influences of the kingdom of grace are not less reciprocal and effective. A Christian poet has so happily and beautifully expressed this sentiment, that we venture to close this introduction with its quotation, commending in fervent prayer this volume and its reader to the especial blessing and favour of Israel's Triune Jehovah, the Father, Son, and Holy Ghost. Amen.

> *Is thy cruse of comfort wasting?*
>   *Rise and share it with another,*
> *And through all the years of famine,*
>   *It shall serve thee and thy brother:*
> *Love divine will fill thy storehouse,*
>   *Or thy handful still renew;*
> *Scanty fare for one will often*
>   *Make a royal feast for two.*

For the heart grows rich in giving;
All its wealth is living grain;
Seeds (which mildew in the garner)
Scatter'd, fill with gold the plain.
Is thy burden hard and heavy?
Do thy steps drag wearily?
Help to bear thy brother's burden;
God will bear both it and thee.

Numb and weary on the mountains,
Wouldst thou sleep amidst the snow?
Chafe that frozen form beside thee,
And together both shall glow.
Art thou stricken in life's battle?
Many wounded round thee moan;
Lavish on their wounds thy balsams,
And that balm shall heal thine own.

Is the heart a well left empty?
None but God its void can fill;
Nothing but a ceaseless Fountain
Can its ceaseless longings still.
Is the heart a living power?
Self-entwined its strength sinks low;
It can only live in loving,
And by serving love will grow.

— Octavius Winslow

BATH, *August* 1860.

CHAPTER 1

The Ransomed Returning Home

And the ransomed of the LORD shall return, and come to Zion with songs and everlasting joy upon their heads: they shall obtain joy and gladness, and sorrow and sighing shall flee away.

— Isaiah 35:10

The children of God are on their way to the Father's house. As spiritual voyagers they are homeward-bound. Heaven is the place at which they will as certainly arrive as that Christ himself is there. Already the expectant of glory binds the 'wave sheaf' to his believing bosom. Faith is the spiritual spy of the soul. It travels far into the promised land, gathers the ripe clusters – the evidences and earnest of its reality and richness – and, returning, bears with it these, the 'first-fruits' of the coming vintage. 'My soul desired the firstripe fruits' (*Mic.* 7:1), and he who has in his soul the 'firstfruits of the Spirit, waiting for the adoption, to wit, the redemption of the body' (*Rom.* 8:23), knows something in his experience of heaven upon earth. Ah! many a glimpse and gleam of the heavenly land dawns upon the Christian in the darkness of his dungeon, in the loneliness of his exile, in the cloistered stillness of his suffering chamber. Such was the rapture of a departing saint:

> The celestial city is full in my view. Its glories beam upon me, its breezes fan me, its odours are wafted to me, its sounds strike upon my ear, and its spirit is breathed into my heart. Nothing separates me from it but the river of death, which now appears but as an insignificant rill, that may be crossed at a single step, whenever God shall give permission. The Sun of Righteousness has been gradually drawing nearer and nearer, appearing larger and brighter as he approached, and now he fills the whole hemisphere, pouring forth a flood of glory, in which I seem to float like an insect in the beams of the sun; exulting, yet almost trembling, while I gaze at the excessive brightness, and wondering with unutterable wonder why God should deign thus to shine upon a sinful worm.

Thus, long ere the believer reaches the celestial city, the evidences of its existence and fertility float past his barque, as manifestly as did the tokens of a new world the vessel which bore Columbus to its shores. The relation of present grace to future glory is close and indissoluble. It is that of the seed to the flower, of the morning twilight to meridian day. Grace is the germ of glory; glory is the highest perfection of grace. Grace is glory militant; glory is grace triumphant. Thus the believer has two heavens to enjoy, a present heaven experienced in the love of God in his heart, and a future heaven in the fulness of joy that is at Christ's right hand, and the pleasures that are for evermore. We wish not at this stage of our work to introduce the dark background of the picture, and yet we cannot withhold the passing remark, that as *heaven* has its foretastes of happiness, its prelibations of glory, its dayspring from on high in the heart of the regenerate, so has *hell* its dark forebodings, its certain approaches, in the soul of many of the unregenerate – some shadows of the 'outer darkness' that will enshroud the lost forever. Reader, is it heaven or hell of which you have in your experience the earnest? One drop of hell, one beam of heaven, can fill the soul with either!

And yet, though journeying homeward, we are but slow voyagers. Our barque often slumbers upon its shadow, as if anchored motionless in the still, calm waters within the haven, instead of cleaving the mighty billows and speeding its way in full sail for the everlasting kingdom. Alas! how few there are who have an 'abundant entrance' into the kingdom of grace below. They are, at best, but hangers upon the door of the ark, but borderers upon the land that freely flows with the fulness of a full Christ. Like Israel of old they 'possess not their possessions'. There is much of the good land they have never explored. Much peace, much joy, much love, much hope, much in an advanced knowledge of Christ and of God, and of their interest in the Saviour's love and in the high and heavenly calling, is attainable, but to which they have not attained; they have not apprehended that for which they are apprehended of Christ Jesus. They are heard more often mournfully to exclaim, 'My soul cleaveth unto the dust' (*Psa.* 119:25), rather than in the more joyful strains, 'O that I had wings like a dove! for then would I fly away, and be at rest' (*Psa.* 55:6). To help your soul heavenward, to point the steps by which you may ascend nearer to God and advance with quickened speed towards your eternal rest, to encourage, cheer, and stimulate, we proceed to expound the appropriate truths and to unveil the winning hopes, by which the gospel of Christ seeks to promote our heavenly meetness and to allure us to a world of perfect and endless bliss. We can scarcely select from the Word of God, as illustrating the character, the journey, and the prospects of the believer, a more striking and beautiful portion than that which we propose in the present chapter to open: 'And the ransomed of the LORD shall return, and come to Zion with songs and everlasting joy upon their heads: they shall obtain joy and gladness, and sorrow and sighing shall flee away' (*Isa.* 35:10).

It is a most beautiful, expressive delineation of the character of the Lord's people, *the ransomed of the LORD*. Mark how the Holy Ghost, whether speaking amidst the twilight of the Old, or in the meridian light of the New Testament, ever makes the cross of Christ the grand central truth. Here is a designation which involves great principles and defines a distinct and separate condition of our humanity. It casts into the deepest shade earth's proudest titles, eclipses the glory of all intellectual greatness, and outbids the world's dearest delights. Bring all the objects of sense, and all the discoveries of science, and all the achievements of intellect, and all the fame and distinction and glory for which heroes ever sighed, or which senators ever won, and place it in focal power side by side with the salvation of the soul, and it pales into insignificance. But let us, in a few words, open up this high character – the 'ransomed of the LORD'.

The word implies a previous state of bondage, slavery, and servitude. We speak properly of redeeming a captive, of ransoming a slave. Now the 'ransomed of the LORD' are delivered from just such a state. By nature we are bond-slaves, the servants of sin, the captives of Satan. Christ's redemption changes this state; it ransoms and emancipates the church. It totally reverses our moral condition. It makes a freeman of a slave; a child of an alien; a friend of a foe; a saint of a sinner; an heir of heaven of an heir of hell. The atoning work of Christ brings us back to our original and unfallen state, while it advances us in dignity, glory, and safety transcendently beyond it. We receive by the second Adam all, and infinitely more than we lost in the first Adam. But look at the leading points in this process of redemption. The Ransomer is God, the ransom price is the vicarious sacrifice of Jesus, the ransomed are the whole election of grace. How striking the words of Jehovah, 'Deliver him from going down to the pit: I have found a ransom' (*Job* 33:24). It is the gracious exclamation of the Father. *He* provides the ransom. He found it reposing from eternity in his own bosom; he found it in himself, 'God will provide himself a lamb for a burnt offering' (*Gen.* 22:8). Thus does the New Testament confirm the Old, while the Old Testament foreshadows the New. 'Whom God hath set forth to be a propitiation through faith in his blood' (*Rom.* 3:25). 'God so loved the world, that he gave his only begotten Son' (*John* 3:16).

Do not fail, beloved reader, to trace up your gracious springs to their infinite fountain, God's everlasting love. To stop at Calvary is to trace the river but halfway to its source. We admit that the spiritual traveller arriving at the cross finds a new world of grandeur bursting upon his view; but as he pursues his research and learns more of the character, and heart, and purpose of God in salvation, there unfolds to his eye an expanse of moral scenery, clad in such tenderness, unveiling such sublimity, and vocal with such song, as infinitely transcends his loftiest thought or conception of the character, government, and glory of Jehovah. The cross is the only stand-point, and Christ is the only mirror, where God can be rightly studied and seen.

From this glance at the Father, the originating source of our ransom, turn we for a moment to the Ransomer. No other being could have achieved the work but Jesus. No other ransomer was divine enough, nor holy enough, nor strong enough, nor loving enough. He was just the Ransomer for God, and just the ransom for man. Reposing one hand upon the throne of heaven and the other upon the cross of earth, by the sacrifice of himself he so united and reconciled God and man. Henceforth the *cross* and the *throne* are one, and will form the study, admiration, and praise of unfallen and redeemed intelligences through eternity. How clearly the apostle puts this fact of our reconciliation! 'And, having made peace through the blood of his cross, by him to reconcile all things unto himself; by him, I say, whether they be things in earth, or things in heaven. And you, that were sometime alienated and enemies in your mind by wicked works, yet now hath he reconciled in the body of his flesh through death, to present you holy and unblameable and unreprovable in his sight' (*Col.* 1:20–22).

And whence this costly and precious offering? The Word of God alone can supply the answer: 'Herein is love!' Love eternal moved the heart of Christ to relinquish heaven for earth, a diadem for a cross, the robe of divine majesty for the garment of our nature, taking *upon* himself the leprosy of our sin, while *in* him was no sin at all. Oh the infinite love of Christ! What a boundless, fathomless ocean! Never was there, and never can there be, in the highest development of the affections, *such* love as Christ's. Ask the 'ransomed of the LORD', whose chains he has dissolved, whose dungeon he has opened, whose liberty he has conferred, whose music angels bend to hear, if there ever was love like his! This is the love, beloved, we are so prone to question in our trials, to quench in our sorrows, to limit in our difficulties, and to lose sight of under the pressure of guilt and in the writhings of divine correction. Oh, whatever else you question, whatever else you doubt, question not, doubt not the love that Jesus, your Ransomer, bears you!

And what shall we say of the *ransom price?* It was the richest, the costliest, heaven could give. 'He gave himself for us.' What more could he do? What less would have sufficed? It were, perhaps, an easy sacrifice for an individual to give his time, or his property, or his influence, or the expression of his sympathy for an object; but to give himself, to sell himself into slavery, or to immolate himself as a sacrifice, were quite another thing. The Son of God gave not angels, of whom he was Lord; nor men, of whom he was the Creator; nor the world, of which he was the Proprietor; but he gave *himself* – body, spirit, soul, his time, his labour, his blood, his life, his death, his all, as the price of our ransom, as the cost of our redemption. He carried the wood, and he reared the altar; then, baring his bosom to the stroke of the uplifted and descending arm of the Father, paid the price of our salvation in the warm lifeblood of his heart. The law exclaimed, 'I am honoured!' Justice said, 'I am satisfied!' 'Mercy and truth are met together; righteousness and peace have kissed each other' (*Psa.* 85:10), and heaven resounded with hallelujahs. 'Ye are bought with a price' (*1 Cor.* 7:23); and *what* a price, O Christian! 'Ye were not redeemed with corruptible things, as silver and gold, but with the precious blood of Christ' (*1 Pet.* 1:18–19). Bear about with you the vivid remembrance of this truth, that your whole life may be a holy thing, a pleasant psalm of thanksgiving and praise to God. How potent the argument, how touching the motive! 'I am a ransomed being; I am the price of blood, the blood of the incarnate Deity; *therefore*, and henceforth, I am to glorify him in my body, soul, and spirit, who redeemed, disenthralled, and saved me.'

How is it that we feel the force and exemplify the practical influence of this amazing, all-commanding truth so faintly? Oh the desperate depravity of our nature! Oh the deep iniquity of our iniquitous hearts! Will not the blood drops of Jesus move us? Will not the unknown agonies of the cross influence us? Will not his dying love constrain us to a more heavenly walk? Ransomed from the curse, from sin, and from Satan, brought out of Egypt with a high and outstretched arm, surely this should speed us onward, quicken our progress heavenward, and constrain us, with Moses, 'esteeming the reproach of Christ greater riches than the treasures of Egypt: for he had respect unto the recompense of the reward' (*Heb.* 11:26). How ought we to 'lay aside every weight, and the sin which doth so easily beset us, and let us run with patience the race that is set before us, looking unto Jesus' (*Heb.* 12:1–2), and so speed our way to the heavenly city!

We need scarcely remind the reader that the 'ransomed of the LORD' compose the whole election of grace, the one Church of Christ, and the one family of God. What a uniting, sanctifying, and heaven-helping truth is this! The divisions which divide and separate the Church of God are human; the ties which bind and unite the Church of God are divine. The many systems of ecclesiastical polity and modes of worship, which present to the eye the Christian Church as a 'house divided against itself' (*Matt.* 12:25), are of man; but the affection and sympathy, the doctrines and the hopes, which create an essential oneness in the family and domesticate the habits and conversation of its members, are of God, and because they are of God, they shall never be destroyed. This truth is a heaven-helping truth. That which promotes our holiness promotes our heavenliness; and growing heavenliness advances us nearer to heaven. If we walked more in love and fellowship and sympathy with the Lord's people of each part of the one fold, we should have a sweeter cross and a lighter burden to carry. Are we not making more real and rapid progress in our heavenly course and in meetness for heaven itself, when by love we are serving one another, rather than when in the bitterness of a bigoted and sectarian spirit we wrangle and dispute, 'bite and devour one another' (*Gal.* 5:15)? Try the power of love, beloved reader, lay aside the prejudice, suspicion, and coldness which divide you in fellowship and labour from other Christian communions than your own, and see if you may not, by sacred intercourse, mutual faith, prayer, service, and sympathy, gather the strength and the encouragement that shall accelerate and smooth your heavenward way. No grace advances the soul with greater force towards a heaven of love than love itself – whether it be love to man, or love to God who redeemed man. 'The love of Christ constraineth us' (2 *Cor.* 5:14).

And now let us consider the *return home* of the Lord's ransomed; this truth will bring the beaming prospect of the Church of God more closely before us. 'The ransomed of the LORD *shall return, and come to Zion*' (*Isa.* 35:10). The Church of God in her Babylonish captivity, hanging her harp upon the willows that drooped over the waters in which she mingled her tears, with her captivity turned and brought again to Zion, is an impressive symbol of the Christian Church. We are in Babylon now, and prisoners of hope. But we shall return from our captivity ere long and come to the heavenly Zion. Earth shall not always be our place of exile; we shall not always sing the Lord's song in a strange land, nor always shed these tears and wear these fetters and endure these cruel taunts of our foes. Each trembling step of faith, each holy aspiration of love, each sin subdued, each foe vanquished, each trial past, each temptation baffled, is bringing us nearer and still nearer to the bright threshold of glory, upon which sister spirits stand beckoning us home.

Oh yes, we shall return! We shall return from our first departure from our Father, from our exile from Paradise, from the strange land into which we were driven, from all our heart and household idols, from all our treacherous departures and base backslidings, from all our secret and open conflicts, from all our veiled and visible sorrows, from all that taints and wounds and shades us now. Every wanderer shall return – the lamb that strayed from the Shepherd's side, the sheep that broke from the fold, the child that forsook the Father's home – all, all shall return, 'kept by the power of God' (1 Pet. 1:5), secured by the everlasting covenant, restored and brought back by the unchanging love and faithfulness of the ever-living Head and enthroned High Priest within the veil. All shall return.

But one element of bliss yet remains to complete and consummate this return of the ransomed of the Lord. We refer to the *final resurrection of the body*. We do not adopt the frigid idea, as maintained by some, of an intermediate state intervening between the present happiness of

the saints and the resurrection of the body, during which
the soul remains in a state of dreamy repose and not in
the full play of its perfected and enlarged powers, bask-
ing in the warm sunshine of the divine glory. We rather
adopt what we conceive is the more scriptural and pleasant idea of the believing soul's immediate entrance into
the glorified presence, that 'absent from the body [is] to
be present with the Lord' (2 Cor. 5:8). But we hold, at the
same time, that the happiness and the glory of the saints
are not complete until the ransomed soul is once more
the occupant of the ransomed body, and that this reun-
ion transpires on the morning of the 'first resurrection'.
This truth is written upon the page of God's Word as
with a sunbeam. What saith the Lord by the mouth of
the prophet? 'I will ransom them from the power of the
grave; I will redeem them from death: O death, I will be
thy plagues; O grave, I will be thy destruction' (Hos.
13:14). And again, 'Thy dead men shall live, together
with my dead body shall they arise. Awake and sing, ye
that dwell in dust: for thy dew is as the dew of herbs,[1]
and the earth shall cast out the dead' (Isa. 26:19). How
strong was Job's faith in the glorious resurrection: 'I
know that my redeemer liveth, and that he shall stand at
the latter day upon the earth: and though after my skin
worms destroy this body, yet in my flesh shall I see God'
(Job 19:25–26). Then comes the full redemption, the re-
espousal of the ransomed body and the ransomed soul,
both now identically and eternally one, celebrating the
'marriage supper of the Lamb' (Rev. 19:9)!

Glorious as the resurrection will be to all, especially

---

[1]In Hebrew, 'Awake and sing, ye that dwell in the dust! Behold,
the dew of daylight is thy dew.'

glorious will it be to some of the saints. Their frames, now distorted by nature, paralyzed by disease, wasted by sickness, shall then feel the quickening touch of Christ – gentle as a mother's kiss waking her infant from its slumber – and spring from the dust a spiritual body, refined and etherealized, vigour in every limb, symmetry in every proportion, grace in every motion, perfection in every sense. Blindness shall no more dim the eye, nor deafness blunt the hearing – clad in a robe of light, rivalling the splendour of an angel's form, holiness sanctifying, and immortality enshrining the whole. Shall this be thought by you a thing incredible? He who is the 'resurrection and the life' will accomplish it. His word is given, his power is engaged, his glory is involved, and his own resurrection is a pledge and 'firstfruits' that he 'shall change our vile body, that it may be fashioned like unto his glorious body, according to the working whereby he is able even to subdue all things unto himself' (*Phil.* 3:21).

And whither shall we return? '*To Zion.*' That Zion which John saw and described: 'And I looked, and, lo, a Lamb stood on the mount Sion, and with him an hundred forty and four thousand, having his Father's name written in their foreheads' (*Rev.* 14:1). And still the Lamb is the central object, whatever the apocalyptic vision John beheld. Jesus is ever in the midst of his churches, his golden candlesticks, standing up in his divine majesty, and in his invincible strength, for the children of his people. Around him cluster his ransomed ones, all sealed in their foreheads, open, and manifest, and visible to all, with the new name which adoption gives, whereby they cry 'Abba, Father'.

Then, there is the *music* with which the ransomed of

the Lord shall return to Zion: 'with songs and everlasting joy upon their heads' (*Isa.* 35:10). The songs of the believer are often mingled with sighs and groans in this vale of tears; it is a blended song we sing, of 'mercy and of judgment'. But no harsh discordant notes will mar this new-born anthem. We shall sweep no strings that jar, and touch no chords that respond not to the entire compass of the musical tones of glory. Joy, now sadly interrupted, will then wreath our brow as a diadem. Chanting music, crowned with joy, we shall take our places with the sealed of God on Mount Zion.

'Sorrow and sighing shall flee away' (*Isa.* 35:10). What expressive and joyous words are these! Sorrow without and sighing within make up much of our checkered experience here on earth. What a blended history is ours! We commence our day with a heart freshly tuned, breathing its morning hymn of praise so sweetly; but ere the sun that rose so brightly is set, what shadows have deepened around our soul! We lay an aching head upon our pillow, thankful that the blood of sprinkling cleanseth from all sin. But from the heaven to which we are going, all sorrow and sighing will forever have passed. The shadows will have dissolved, sin will be effaced, sighing will cease, sorrow will be turned into 'fulness of joy', and heaven will be resplendent with undimmed and unfading glory and resound with a new and endless song. Is not this heaven worth living for, worth suffering for, worth labouring for – nay, if need be, worth a thousand martyrdoms?

A captive here, and far from home,
For Zion's sacred courts I sigh:
Thither the ransom'd nations come,
And see the Saviour eye to eye.

While here, I walk on hostile ground;
    The few that I can call my friends
Are, like myself, with fetters bound,
    And weariness my path attends.

But we shall soon behold the day
    When Zion's children shall return;
Our sorrows then shall flee away,
    And we shall never, never mourn.

The hope that such a day will come
    Makes e'en the captive's portion sweet;
Though now we're distant far from home,
    In Zion soon we all shall meet.

CHAPTER 2

Progressive Meetness for Heaven

And I will send hornets before thee, which shall drive out the Hivite, the Canaanite, and the Hittite, from before thee. I will not drive them out from before thee in one year; lest the land become desolate, and the beast of the field multiply against thee. By little and little I will drive them out from before thee, until thou be increased, and inherit the land.

— Exodus 23:28–30

Sanctification, or heavenly meetness, is an initial work in the great process by which God prepares the soul for glory. Justification, that instantaneous act of his free grace by which the soul is brought into a state of divine acceptance, is a present and a complete work. The moment a believing sinner receives Christ and is clothed upon with his imputed righteousness, that moment he is in possession of the divine title-deed to the inheritance of the saints in light. Thus, justification, because it is an *imputed*, and sanctification, because it is an *imparted* act, though cognate doctrines, are distinct works and must not be considered as identical, as the Roman Catholics and many Protestants have done. By one act of faith in

Christ we are justified; but it is by a gradual work of the Spirit that we are sanctified. It is a solemn declaration, 'Holiness, without which no man shall see the Lord' (*Heb.* 12:14). There is no vision of God either present or future, save through the medium of holiness. A holy God can only be seen with an enlightened and sanctified eye. The spiritual vision must be 'anointed with eye-salve'. The divine Oculist must couch the moral cataract, must remove the film of sin, ignorance, and prejudice from the mental eye, ere one ray of divine holiness can dart in upon the retina of the soul. As one born blind cannot see the sun, so the soul morally blind cannot see God. Therefore our Lord said to Nicodemus, 'Except a man be born again, he cannot see the kingdom of God' (*John* 3:3). He cannot see it, because he is not a subject of the new and second birth. We have remarked that this work of holiness is initiatory, and therefore not complete. It is real, but progressive; certain, but gradual; and although in a moment, in the twinkling of an eye, God can fit the believer for heaven, it yet goes forward little and by little until it reaches the culminating point, and then the door of glory opens and receives to its bosom the soul fitted for its purity and bliss.

In supplying the reader with a few helps heavenward, we plant his feet upon one of the lowest rungs of the ladder, when we, at this early stage of our subject, direct his thoughts to *progressive meetness for heaven*. And we the more advisedly and earnestly do this because of the crude and imperfect views of heavenliness which many, especially young Christians, entertain, and in consequence of which are involved in much legality of mind and distress of soul. We have selected, as illustrating this important doctrine, an incident in the early settlement of the Israelites in Canaan. It was God's arrangement that they should colonize the land amidst its many and idolatrous inhabitants; who, so far from sympathizing with their habits and worship, presented an antagonistic and formidable aspect: so that, while it was a land of rest and affluence, it was yet a scene of perpetual invasion and conflict, demanding on their part the watchful eye and the furbished weapon. Now the God who planted them in the promised land could as easily have exterminated their foes; but not so, for reasons which his wisdom would dictate and which his goodness would justify, he permitted the inhabitants to continue in possession, until, by a process gradual and progressive, Canaan should be decimated of its idolatrous population, and his own people should go up into its length and breadth and fully possess the land which the Lord their God gave them. 'By little and little I will drive them out from before you' (*Exod.* 23:30). How strikingly are the two cognate yet distinct doctrines of the glorious gospel – justification and sanctification – illustrated here. The planting of the children of Israel in Canaan illustrates the present justification of the Church of God; their protracted conquest of the land illustrates the gradual subjugation of the believer's sinfulness to the supremacy of holiness, or, in other words, his progressive meetness for heaven.

Now let us trace more fully the analogy between this part of Israel's history, and the spiritual experience of the Church of God and of every individual member of that Church. Oh that the divine Spirit may be our Teacher, his grace our anointing, Christ the first, the centre, and the last, and our advanced meetness for heaven the personal and happy result of our meditation upon this sacred truth! And if, child of God, heaven shall be brought nearer to your soul and your soul's meetness for heaven be promoted, we shall thank our heavenly Father for this advanced step; and, strengthened and cheered, we shall seek another and yet another, and so ascend, until, reaching the highest rung, we find ourselves in heaven.

Canaan was a land of *rest:* it was that good land in which the Israelites were to terminate their long and wearisome march in sweet and delightsome repose. The moment a poor believing soul is brought to Jesus, he is brought to rest. 'We which have believed do enter into rest' (*Heb.* 4:3). The instant that he crosses the border that separates the covenant of works from the covenant of grace, the moment that he emerges from the wilderness of his doings and toil – his going about to establish a righteousness of his own – and enters believingly into Christ, he is at rest. The true Joshua has brought him into Canaan, has brought him to himself; and his long travelling, weary soul is at peace with God through Christ. 'For he that is entered into his rest, he also hath ceased from his own works, as God did from his' (*Heb.* 4:10). Behold the rest! It is Jesus. His finished work, his blood and righteousness, his law-fulfilling obedience, and his justice-satisfying death, give perfect rest from guilt and condemnation and sorrow to him that simply enters, though it be but a border-touch of faith, into Jesus.

Oh, art thou a sin-burdened, a wilderness-wearied soul? Art thou seeking rest in the law, in convictions of sin, in pious duties, in churches and sacraments? Each one exclaims, 'It is not in me!' Turn from these, and bend your listening ear to the gentle voice of your gracious Saviour, 'Come unto me, all ye that labour and are heavy

laden, and I will give you rest' (*Matt.* 11:28). What wondrous words are these! Tell me not that you are too sinful
and unworthy to come; that you are too vile to lay your
head upon that sacred bosom; too guilty to bathe in that
cleansing stream; too poor to clothe you in that divine
righteousness. I reply, Jesus bids you come. Can you,
dare you refuse? The instant that you cease to labour,
and enter believingly, savingly into Christ, that instant you
are safe within the City of Refuge, beyond the reach of sin,
and condemnation, and the law's curse, and the uplifted
arm of the avenger of blood. 'Being justified by faith, we
have peace with God through our Lord Jesus Christ' (*Rom.*
5:1). Note the present tense here: we *have* peace.

But notwithstanding this perfect state of pardon, justification, and rest, into which the believing soul is
brought, is sin utterly and totally extirpated from his
bosom? In other words, because forgiveness is complete
and acceptance is complete, is *sanctification* complete? Far
from it, beloved. It is a good land and a wealthy, a land of
peace and rest, into which grace has led us, but it is, nevertheless, a land besieged by foes – for the Canaanites still
dwell therein – and of consequent warfare. The believer
has to fight his way to heaven. In the soul, in the centre
of the very heart where perfect rest and peace are experienced, there dwell innate and powerful corruptions,
ever invading our peaceful possessions, seeking to dis-
turb our repose and to bring us into subjection. 'O
wretched man that I am! who shall deliver me from the
body of this death?' (*Rom.* 7:24)

Observe, too, these inhabitants of the land inter-
posed a powerful barrier between the Israelites and their
full possession. They were at best but borderers. They had
indeed passed the confines of the desert and pressed the

soil of the promised land, but how small a portion of the vast territory did they as yet occupy! Far beyond them, stretching in luxuriant beauty, were vine-clad hills, and flowing rivers, acres of wheat and barley and pomegranates, fountains and depths that spring out of valleys which they had not as yet explored.

Is not this a picture of our spiritual state? How much interposes between us and our spiritual possessions! What keeps us from the 'abundant entrance' into the kingdom of grace, but our ever-present and ever-sleepless enemy, unbelief? What prevents a more full and cordial acceptance of the righteousness of Christ, but a constant dealing with our own unrighteousness? What keeps us from enjoying more of heaven upon earth, but the too-absorbing influence of the world? What causes us to live so far below the privilege of our high vocation, dwarfs our Christianity, lowers our profession, shades the lustre and impairs the vigour of our holy religion, but the depravity, the corruption, the sin that dwells in us? These are the spiritual Canaanites which prevent our going up to possess the good land in its length and breadth. What an evidence this is, that though our Lord Jesus has put us into a state of present and complete acceptance, we have not as yet attained unto a state of perfect and future holiness – the Canaanites still dwell in the land! We are called to 'fight the good fight of faith' (*1 Tim.* 6:12). Not only do we war with flesh and blood, but we wrestle 'against principalities, against powers, against the rulers of the darkness of this world, against spiritual wickedness in high places' (*Eph.* 6:12).

But why should this thwart our advance? Why should the existence and ever-threatening attitude of our foes prevent us from living upon a full Christ, a present Christ, a loving Christ, day by day, hour by hour, moment by moment? Clad in our invincible armour, why should we not carve our way through the serried ranks of our foes and penetrate into the heart of Canaan, pluck thence the grapes, gather the honey, drink of the fountains, and explore the hidden things which God has treasured for us in the covenant of grace, in the fulness of our Surety Head, in the infinite greatness of his own love, and in the unsearchable riches of his gospel, his revealed truth? Oh, how much of the good land remains yet to be possessed! Truly, 'eye hath not seen, nor ear heard, neither have entered into the heart of man, the things which God hath prepared for them that love him' (*1 Cor.* 2:9). Well might the grateful psalmist exclaim, and each believer in Jesus respond, 'O how great is thy goodness, which thou hast laid up for them that fear thee' (*Psa.* 31:19)!

There is one view of this truth exceedingly helpful to Zion's travellers; we refer to the fact that God is never unmindful of the trying and critical position of his people, dwelling in the midst of their enemies, and their enemies dwelling in the midst of them. He knows all your corruptions, your infirmities, your besetting sin, weakness, and frailty. He has, too, his unslumbering eye upon all the stratagems and assaults of Satan, never for an instant losing sight of or ceasing to control and check this subtle and sleepless foe. Never does thy Lord forget that the body he has redeemed is yet a 'body of sin and death' and that the soul he has ransomed with his most precious blood is still the seat of principles, passions, and thoughts inimical to its perfect holiness and ever seeking to subjugate it to the body.

Did not Jesus recognize this truth when he said to his disciples, 'Behold, I send you forth as sheep in the midst of wolves' (*Matt.* 10:16)? What expressive words! *Sheep* in the midst of *wolves*! Who can save them? The Shepherd who gave his life for them, the 'Lion of the tribe of Judah' – he will keep, shield, and preserve them. Oh, take the encouragement and comfort which this truth gives, that your Lord knows your exposure to and your conflict with the enemies of the land! You have on your side, allied with you in this spiritual warfare, his loving heart, his watchful eye, his outstretched arm, and all his legions of angels sent forth to encircle you with chariots of fire. Ah! the world may taunt you with your infirmities, the saints may chide you for your haltings, your own heart may condemn you for its secret declensions, but God, your Father, is very sympathetic and remembers that you are dust; and Jesus, your Advocate, is very compassionate and prays for you within the veil. The saints judge, the world censures, the heart is self-abased; but Christ says, 'Neither do I condemn thee: go, and sin no more' (*John* 8:11).

But we have the promise of *conquest*. God assured the Israelites that he would drive out the Canaanites from before them. Have we an assurance less emphatic or a hope less joyous? What is the promise of this, which appears one of the brightest constellations in the glorious galaxy of the 'exceeding great and precious promises' of God (2 *Pet.* 1:4)? It is, 'He will turn again, he will have compassion upon us; he will subdue our iniquities; and thou wilt cast all our sins into the depths of the sea' (*Mic.* 7:19). What a largess, what an accumulation of blessings, what blest encouragement and heart-cheer to the downcast traveller! 'He will turn again.' Again! He has turned his loving eye, his out-stretched hand, a thousand times over; what! will he 'turn *again*'? After all my baseness and ingratitude; my sins without *confession;* my confession without *repentance;* my repentance without *forsaking;* my forsakings so reluctant, so partial, and so short – what! will he turn to me again, bend upon me once more that loving eye, that forgiving look, that dissolves my heart at his feet? Oh, who is a God like unto thee? And when he turns again, what will he do? He will drive out the Canaanites from before us. In other words, 'He will subdue our iniquities'. What encouragement this is to fall down at his feet – the feet that never spurned a humble suppliant – and cry with his people of old, 'Lord, we have no might against this great company that cometh against us; neither know we what to do: but our eyes are upon thee' (2 *Chron.* 20:12). With such faith and such an appeal, what sin will not God pardon, what iniquity will not Christ subdue, against what confederate host will not the Spirit of the Lord lift up a standard?

But let us not mistake our true position in this holy contest. It is both aggressive and defensive. The children of Israel were not to allow the inhabitants of the land to remain intact. They were to go up armed and drive back the foe. Thus is it with us. When our Lord, the 'Prince of peace', commanded, 'He that hath no sword, let him sell his garment, and buy one' (*Luke* 22:36), he doubtless intended that as significant for the spiritual conflict in which they were to be engaged; for the temporal sword he never authorized in defence or propagation of his truth. We are to be aggressive upon the territory of sin and of error, of ignorance and of the world. To these confederate hosts – the Canaanites of the church – we are to

present a bold, united, antagonistic front. The Bible no-
where ignores, but on the contrary, everywhere
recognizes, the individual responsibility of the Christian.
What means the exhortation, 'Put on the whole armour
of God' (*Eph.* 6:11)? What means the injunction, 'Work
out your own salvation with fear and trembling' (*Phil.*
2:12)? What but that, dwelling in an enemy's land – the
Canaanite, and the Amorite, and the Hittite, and the Per-
izzite, the Hivite and the Jebusite, all combined against us
– we are to 'resist unto blood, striving against sin', and 'to
fight the good fight of faith', to 'keep the body under, and
bring it into subjection', to 'overcome the world', to 'resist
the devil', to 'keep ourselves in the love of God' and 'having done all, to stand' with girded loins, waiting and
watching for the coming of our Captain.

O child of God, be not cast down and discouraged in
this holy war! The Lord, he it is that fights for you. By
prayer, by vigilance, by the sword of the Spirit, which is
the Word of God, by keeping out of temptation, by dou-
bling the picket where you are the most exposed to the
invasion of the foe, above all, by bearing your conflicts to
Christ, linking your weakness with his strength, your infirmity with his grace, the erring of your heart, the
faltering of your feet, the hidden conflict of your mind
and will with evil, to his most tender, most reasonable,
most forgiving love; thus will he teach your hands to
war and your fingers to fight, and thus shall you exclaim, 'I can do all things through Christ which
strengtheneth me' (*Phil.* 4:13).

We have arrived now at a deeply interesting and instructive part of this chapter, the *progressive meetness* of
the believer for heaven. 'By little and little I will drive
them out from before thee'. If it so pleased him, God

could as instantaneously mature our sanctification as he perfects our justification. By one stroke of his arm he could have extirpated the idolatrous inhabitants of Canaan and have caused his flock to lie down in quiet places. But it was his wisdom, love, and glory that they should be driven out 'by little and little'. We must resolve the circumstance of God's permissive will touching the indwelling of sin in the believer into the same view of his character. His wisdom appoints it; his will permits it; his love controls it. Where would be the display of his grace and power in the soul as it is now exhibited in the daily life of a child of God, but for the existence of a nature partially sanctified? How little should we learn of the mysteries of the life of faith, how imperfectly skilled in the heavenly war, how stagnant the well of living water within us, how dwarfed and paralyzed every grace of the soul, how partial our knowledge of God, how little our acquaintance with Christ, how small a measure of the indwelling power of the Holy Ghost, how little holy wrestling with the Angel of the Covenant, how faint the incense of prayer, and how distant and dim an object to our spiritual vision the cross of Christ, but for the gradual subduing of our iniquities, the driving from before us 'by little and little' our corruptions, the progressive advance of the soul in its holy, sanctified meetness for heaven!

Yes, it is 'by little and little' this holy work is done. Here the power of sin is weakened, there the spell of a temptation is broken; here an advancing foe is foiled, there a deep-laid plot is discovered; and thus 'by little and little', by a gradual process, aggressive and defensive, of spiritual encounter and extermination, the spiritual Canaanites are subdued and the soul becomes 'meet to be partakers of the inheritance of the saints in light' (*Col.* 1:12).

The subject presented in this chapter is replete with instruction, encouragement, and help heavenward. Many of the Lord's people are looking for the full, the complete sanctification which the Lord has not appointed here and which is only attained when the last bond of corruption is severed. The more deeply the children of Israel explored the good land, the more intelligently and experimentally they became acquainted with the number and power of their enemies. Thus it is we are taught. Ignorance of our own heart, a false idea of the strength of our corruption, a blind, undue estimate of the number and tact of our indwelling sins, is not favourable to our growth in holiness. But the Holy Spirit leads us deeper and deeper into self-knowledge, shows us more and more of the hidden evil, unveils by little and little the chamber of imagery, teaches us 'line upon line; here a little, and there a little' (*Isa.* 28:10); and thus, by a gradual and progressive process, we are made meet for glory.

Are you, beloved reader, like the children of Israel, conscious of impoverishment by the marauding incursions of the enemy? Then, do as they did, cry unto the Lord. Thus we read, 'And Israel was greatly impoverished because of the Midianites; and the children of Israel cried unto the Lord' (*Judg.* 6:6). Oh, besiege the throne of grace, and your foes shall be driven back! Cry mightily unto Jesus, your Commander and Leader, the Captain of your salvation, and he will defeat their plots and deliver you from their power. Tell him that you hate sin and loathe yourselves because of its existence and taint. Tell him you long to be holy, pant to be delivered from the last remnant of corruption, and that the heavenly voice that bids you unclasp your wings and soar to a world of perfect purity will be the sweetest and the dearest that ever chimed upon your ear. O blessed moment! With what splendour has the hand of prophecy portrayed it before the eye: 'In that day shall there be upon the bells of the horses, HOLINESS UNTO THE LORD; and the pots in the LORD's house shall be like the bowls before the altar. Yea, every pot in Jerusalem and in Judah shall be holiness unto the LORD of hosts: and all they that sacrifice shall come and take of them, and seethe therein: and in that day there shall be no more the Canaanite in the house of the LORD of hosts' (*Zech.* 14:20–21).

O blessed day when all false doctrine, and all superstitious worship, and all indwelling sin, and all worldly temptation, and all self-seeking, and iniquity of every name, and sorrow of every form, shall be utterly exterminated, and *holiness to the Lord* shall hallow every enjoyment and consecrate every thing, and enshrine every being! Speed, oh speed the day, blessed Redeemer, when every throb of my heart, and every faculty of my mind, and every power of my soul and every aspiration of my lips, and every glance of my eye, yea, every thought and word and deed, shall be *holiness to the Lord*! Oh, precious day of God, when will it arrive?

Shall the lover of Jesus be indeed delivered from all false pastors, all corrupt worship, and the Lord have turned to the people a pure language, that they may all call upon the name of the Lord, to serve him with one consent? Shall my soul indeed be freed, not only from all the sorrows, pains, evils, and afflictions of sin around me, but, what is infinitely better than all, from the very being and indwelling of sin within me? Shall the fountain of corruption, both of original and actual sin, be dried up, so that I shall never think a vain thought, nor speak an idle, sinful word any more? Is there such a day in which the Canaanites shall be wholly driven out? Oh, blessed, precious, precious promise! Oh, dearest Jesus, to what a blessed state hast thou begotten poor sinners of the earth by thy blood and righteousness! Hasten it, Lord. Cut short thy work, thou that art mighty to save, and take thy willing captive home from myself, and all the remaining Canaanites yet in the land, which are the very tyrants of my soul. Welcome, oh welcome, beloved, every circumstance, every dispensation, every trial that speeds you homeward and matures your soul for the heaven of glory Christ has gone to prepare for you! It is 'by little and by little', not all at once, that believers fight the battle and obtain the victory: 'They go from strength to strength, every one of them in Zion appeareth before God' (Psa. 84:7). Your path to glory shall be as the light, shining with ever-growing, ever-deepening, ever-brightening lustre of truth, grace, and holiness, until you find yourself lost amidst the splendours of a perfect and eternal day! Onward, traveller, onward! From an earthly, you are passing to a heavenly Canaan, in which no foe enters and from which no friend departs, where eternity will be prolonged, as time began, in a paradise of perfect purity and love, amidst whose verdant bowers lurks no subtle serpent and along whose sylvan windings treads no ensnaring Eve. Shudder not to pass the Jordan that divides the earthly from the heavenly Canaan. The Ark of the Covenant will go before you, upborne upon the shoulder of your great High Priest, cleaving the waters as you pass and conducting you, gently, softly, and triumphantly, home to God.

I saw an aged pilgrim,
   Whose toilsome march was o'er,
With slow and painful footstep
   Approaching Jordan's shore:
He first his dusty vestment
   And sandals cast aside,
Then, with an air of transport,
   Enter'd the swelling tide.

I thought to see him shudder,
   As cold the waters rose,
And fear'd lest o'er him, surging,
   The murky stream should close;
But calmly and unshrinking,
   The billowy path he trod,
And cheer'd with Jesus' presence,
   Pass'd o'er the raging flood.

On yonder shore to greet him,
   I saw a shining throng;
Some just begun their praising,
   Some had been praising long;
With joy they bade him welcome,
   And struck their harps again,
While through the heavenly arches
   Peal'd the triumphal strain.

Now in a robe of glory,
   And with a starry crown,
I see the weary pilgrim
   With kings and priests sit down;
With prophets, patriarchs, martyrs,
   And saints, a countless throng,
He chants his great deliverance,
   In never-ceasing song.

— Anonymous

CHAPTER 3

The Burdened Gently Led by Christ

He...shall gently lead those that are with young.
— Isaiah 40:11

'Those that are with young' are those that are burdened;
and such are they whom Jesus gently leads. They are a
large portion of the 'little flock' of which Christ is the
Chief Shepherd, Leader, and Exemplar. In nothing
scarcely is the assimilation stronger, and in no particular
more appropriate. It is proper and befitting that the
sheep of the Burden-bearer should themselves be a burdened flock. But little would they know of him as such,
in the glory of his Godhead, in the compassion of his
manhood, in the strength of his shoulders, and in the
tenderness of his heart, but for their wearisome, toilsome
travail. They must be 'with young' to know what the
'gentleness of Christ' is. A general view of our humanity
will present to the eye the spectacle of the whole creation (rational and irrational) groaning and travailing in
pain together until now. Our humanity is a burdened
humanity, and we who believe share that burden in ad-
dition to those of which the unregenerate feel nothing.

Spiritual life renders the soul sensible to many a crushing weight of which the spiritually dead soul is unconscious, just as the corpse feels no pressure. We would not anticipate other portions of this chapter, yet we cannot forbear the remark at this stage that if you discover in your soul that spiritual sensibility, that sense of pain, suffering, and depression produced by a holy consciousness of indwelling evil, of a nature totally depraved, or those diversified spiritual exercises of the soul through which the flock of the Lord's pasture more or less pass, then you have one of the most indubitable evidences of spiritual life. We repeat the remark: it is only a living man who is conscious of the pressure; a corpse cannot feel. Spiritual sensibility is a sign of spiritual life.

The Lord's people, then, find them where you may, in high circles or low, rich or poor, are a burdened people. Each one has his cross, each his load, each his pressure. Oh, how this truth ought to unite the people of God in holy affection, forbearance, and sympathy towards one another! That precept which recognizes the burdens of the Lord's people in the same words also binds them upon our hearts: 'Bear ye one another's burdens, and so fulfil the law of Christ' (*Gal.* 6:2). But let us specify some of the burdens of the Lord's people – those of whom it is said, 'He shall gently lead those that are with young' – and this will prepare us to consider the gentleness of Christ towards them.

All the Lord's people are sensible of the burden of *conscious guilt*. In this particular it may with truth be said that 'He fashioneth their hearts alike' (*Psa.* 33:15). In this school, painful yet needed, all are experimentally taught; and it may be added that from it they never entirely graduate until called home to glory. The lesson of our original and deep sinfulness, the weakness, impurity, and vileness of the flesh, that in it there 'dwelleth no good thing', is the daily, hourly lesson of the Christian's life. If we ever extract any honey from the precious declaration, 'By grace are ye saved', it is under the pressure of our personal and inexpressible vileness and nothingness. Into this bitter cup the Lord distils the sweetness and savour of his most free and rich grace.

But oh, how few people are conscious of this burden, the burden of the curse! And yet it confronts them at every step, meets them in every object, starts up before them at each turn. We cannot gaze upon the outspread landscape, nor walk into the beautiful garden, nor sail upon the lovely lake; we cannot pluck the flowers, nor breathe the air, nor quaff the spring, but the sad, sad truth confronts us, the curse of God has blighted and blasted all! Is man spiritually aware of this? Ah, no! He sighs but knows not why. He is fettered but feels no chain; sickens and knows not the cause. He marvels to find a sepulchre in his garden, disease, decay, and death in such close proximity to his choicest, sweetest, dearest delights. He wonders that his flower fades, that his spring dries, that his sheltering gourd withers in a night. He knows not that the curse is there, that the overshadowing vine breeds its worm. Thus he treads life's short journey from the cradle to the grave crushed beneath this tremendous weight, nor sees as he passes the uplifted cross where Christ was impaled who died to deliver us from its weight, yea, who was 'made a curse for us' (*Gal.* 3:13).

Here and there we see one of this long and gloomy procession awakened to the conviction of the truth and exclaiming, 'What shall I do to be saved?' Here and there we descry a pilgrim with the load upon his back climb the sacred hill and reach the cross, look, and leave his burden and pursue his way, rejoicing in Christ and exclaiming, 'There is now no condemnation' (*Rom.* 8:1)! But the great multitudes pass on insensible and dead.

Not so the Lord's people. Emancipated indeed we are from the curse and condemnation of sin, for Christ our Surety was 'delivered for our offences, and was raised again for our justification' (*Rom.* 4:25); nevertheless, the more healthy our spiritual life, the more frequently and closely the conscience deals with atoning blood, the more alive and sensitive will be our spiritual sensibility to the conviction and pressure of that curse, which, though removed as a condemnation, yet remains as a fact. The tenderness which the blood imparts, the conviction of indebtedness which divine grace gives, deepens the sensibility of sin; and although standing beneath the shadow of the cross and reading our pardon there, the conviction of its exceeding sinfulness is not the less, but all the more, acute. The curse, though removed, has left its lingering shadow upon the soul, and this, to a saint of God, is no little burden. And when to this is added the faltering of the Christian walk, the flaw of service, the imperfection of worship, the dead insect tainting the perfume of the sacred anointing, the dust upon the sandal, the trailed robe, the concealed but not less real and sinful desire of the heart, its foolishness and inconstancy, oh, is there no painfully felt burden in all this to a mind whose moral perceptions are alive and whose spirituality covets the close and holy walk with God?

How keenly sensible, too, are many of God's people of the burden of *bodily infirmity*. The apostle numbers himself among them when, so feelingly and vividly describing this infirmity of the flock, he says, 'We that are in this tabernacle do groan, being burdened' (2 *Cor.* 5:4). While all believers are conscious of this, many are more painfully so than others. Some know not a single day's perfect health, yea, many not an hour's freedom from wearying pain. Days of languor and nights unsoothed by sleep are appointed to them.

Others, while perhaps exempt from positive disease, are afflicted with an acutely nervous, sensitive temperament, subjecting them to a kind of sorrow which compels them to nurse their burden in lonely isolation. It is with them incessant suffering. The trembling of the aspen leaf startles them, their own shadow alarms them, the flutter of an angel's wing as he sweeps past on his mission of love, would discompose them. This is their burden, and usually the last, because the least known of all, to receive the soothing of human kindness, consideration, and sympathy. Christians thus afflicted require a mode of treatment peculiarly patient and gentle. Those who are not conversant with the delicate sensibility of the nervous system can but imperfectly estimate the acute suffering of such. Is it trespassing too curiously into the awful mystery of Christ's unknown agony to venture the surmise that in the terrible conflict which so fearfully agitated his whole frame in the garden as to clothe it with a vesture of blood, there entered deeply this element of suffering – the exquisite sympathy of the nervous system? If this be true, and we see no reason to question it, then how appropriate, precious, and soothing his compassion and sympathy with all his members similarly afflicted! What, beloved, if your case distances the sympathy, or baffles the cure, or even awakens the reproach, of your fellows, let it suffice that every nerve quivering with agony, that every pulse fluttering with excitement, awakens a response of tenderness and sympathy in the Sufferer of Gethsemane. And oh, if this be so, you can well afford to part with a creature's compassion and help, since it but makes room for Christ. Ah, five minutes of experience of his love in the heart is worth more than an eternity of the creature's. And seldom do we think, as we feel the human arm droop, and see the human eye withdrawn, and are conscious of the chill that has crept over the warm bosom upon which we fondly leaned, that Jesus is but preparing us for a more full and entire enthronement of himself in our soul.

Then there are others whose burden is a constant tendency to *mental despondency and gloom*. Whether this is constitutional, is produced by sorrow, or is the result of disease, the effect is the same, a life perpetually cloud-veiled and depressed, scarcely relieved by a transient gleam of sunshine. No little burden is this. 'A mind diseased' involves more real suffering and demands more divine grace than a body diseased. And yet, how large a class is this! What numbers are there of the Lord's people whose spiritual hope is obscured by mental disease, and whose mental disease is, in its turn, produced by some physical irritant – so close is the relation and so sympathetic the emotions of the body and mind. What a mystery is our being! There is one, and but one, who understands it. 'He knoweth our frame; he remembereth that we are dust' (*Psa.* 103:14). Your Saviour, beloved, experienced mental gloom and spiritual depression as you never can. It was not always sunshine and joy with your Lord. His path often wound along the lonely vale, and across the dreary desert, and through the deep gloom of the pathless forest, and he knows the way that you take.

The spiritual despondency of your soul, the cloud-veiling of your mind, the absence of vigorous faith, of heaven-springing joy, and of undimmed hope, do not affect your union with Christ, touch your interest in the love of God, or render doubtful or insecure your place in the many-mansioned house of your Father in heaven. Will not this truth be a little help heavenward? Will not this assurance, founded as it is on the Word of God, distil some joy into your heart, and throw some gleam of sunshine upon your path, and strengthen you as a child of the light to walk through darkness, until you reach that world of glory of which it is said, 'There shall be no night there' (*Rev.* 21:25)? 'Who is among you that feareth the LORD, that obeyeth the voice of his servant, that walketh in darkness, and hath no light? let him trust in the name of the LORD, and stay upon his God' (*Isa.* 50:10). 'Light is sown for the righteous, and gladness for the upright in heart' (*Psa.* 97:11). Take heart and go forward; 'light and gladness' shall spring up in your path just where and when the God who loves you and the Shepherd who leads you sees best. They are 'sown' by God's hand, and they shall spring forth beneath his smile. A covenant-keeping God of unchanging love is bringing you home to himself.

There is often, too, in the experience of many, the burden of some heavy *daily cross*. A personal grief, or a domestic trial, or a family calamity, is the weight they bear, perhaps with not a day's cessation. Is it no burden to have a wounded spirit? Is it no burden to nurse a sorrow which interdicts all human sympathy, which admits not, from its profound depth and sacredness, another to share it? Is it no burden to stand up alone for Jesus and his truth in the domestic circle, allied in the closest

bonds of nature to those concerning whom we must exclaim, 'I am become a stranger unto my brethren, and an
alien unto my mother's children' (*Psa.* 69:8), in whom
your spiritual joy awakens no response, and your spiritual sorrow no sympathy? But, oh, what a privilege and
honour to endure reproach and separation, alienated affection, studied neglect, and relentless persecution, for
Christ's sake! 'And on him they laid the cross, that he
might bear it after Jesus' (*Luke* 23:26). Tried, persecuted
disciple, 'to you it is given, in the behalf of Christ, not
only to believe on him, but also to suffer for his sake'
(*Phil.* 1:29). Unto you Jesus has laid the burden, the
sweet, precious burden, of his cross, that you might bear
it after him. Did ever burden confer such honour, bring
such repose, secure a crown so bright, or lead to such
glory and blessedness? 'Whosoever shall confess me before men, him shall the Son of man also confess before
the angels of God' (*Luke* 12:8). Lord, make thyself more
precious to my heart, then will thy burden be lighter, thy
yoke easier, shame for thee will be sweeter, and thy
cross, rude and heavy though it be, will become increasingly my joy, my glory, and my boast!

Let us now turn our thought to the gentleness with
which the divine Shepherd leads these his burdened
ones, for he 'shall *gently* lead those that are with young'
(*Isa.* 40:11). The Leader is Jesus, the Shepherd. He claims
this as one part of his pastoral office. 'The sheep hear his
voice: and he calleth his own sheep by name, and
leadeth them out' (*John* 10:3). 'He leadeth them out', out
of their unregenerate nature, out of their state of condemnation, out of the world, and out of their families.
And whither does he lead them? He leads them to his
cross, to himself; and, thus accepting and resting in him

as their righteousness, and their salvation, and their portion, he then leads them out to the green pastures he has
provided for the flock, where he causes them to lie
down in safe and quiet resting places. Oh, what a momentous step is this, the first that his people take! To be
led out of our own righteousness and unrighteousness,
out of our wrecked and polluted selves, out of the false
confidences, the spurious hopes, the ritual worship, and
pharisaical religion to which we had been so long and so
fondly wedded, and led to embrace the Lord Jesus as
our one, our sole, our sure hope for eternity; oh, it is
heaven's first, heaven's last and latest step; this step
taken, heaven is sure!

Test your religion, beloved, by this. Has Jesus so
taught you? Has his sovereign grace been exhibited in
leading you out of your worldly circle? His converting
grace in leading you out of your self-righteousness? His
pardoning, justifying grace in leading you to peace, holiness, and hope? Then, if this be so, you are Christ's, and
Christ is yours. Thus does the Lord lead his people. He
leads them through the wilderness, up the steep ascent
and down into the low valley, through water and fire,
cloud and storm, thorn and desert, watching them with
an eye that never slumbers, keeping them by a hand that
never wearies, and encircling them with a love that
never chills. Thus, step by step he leads them on, from
grace to glory, from earth to heaven, from the wilderness
below to the paradise above. Not one of that flock, thus
led, thus guarded, thus loved, shall be missing when the
Shepherd folds them on high. His 'rod and his staff' will
be found to have restored them, guided them, comforted them, and at last to have brought them home.
Little faith, and fickle love, and weak grace, and limited

experience, and defective knowledge, and faltering steps, shall find their way, through trial and temptation and suffering, home to God – not one 'vessel of mercy' missing. Oh, who but Christ could accomplish this? Who but the divine Shepherd could thus have kept, and thus have gathered, and thus have folded the sheep scattered up and down in the cloudy and dark day? What an evidence of the Godhead of Christ! Oh, crown his deity: crown it with your faith, crown it with your love, crown it with your praise, ye who have 'now received the atonement', for nothing short of this could place you within the realms of glory! And this, when there, will be your crown and joy for ever.

The 'gentleness of Christ' is a theme on which the Holy Ghost frequently dwells. It is an essential perfection of his nature. The nature of Christ is gentle. It is not an accident of his being, an engrafted virtue, a cultivated grace; it is essential to his very existence. Recollect that the two natures of our Lord were perfect. If we look at his superior nature, the divine, the wondrous truth meets the eye as if emblazoned in letters of living light, 'God is love'. Now, Christ was an embodiment of the essential love of God; consequently, gentleness was a perfection of his being. If we view his inferior nature, the human, not less manifest was his gentleness, since his humanity, though identified with the curse, and laden with sin, and encompassed with infirmity, and shaded with sorrow, yet was sinless humanity, free from all and the slightest moral taint; and so gentleness in its most exquisite form was one of its most distinguished attributes. If, too, we connect with this truth the fulness of the Spirit in our Lord's human nature, the evidence of its essential and perfect gentleness is complete. And was not the gentleness of Christ visible in his every act? There was nothing censorious in his disposition, nothing harsh in his manner, nothing bitter or caustic in his speech. If with withering rebuke he denounced the hypocrisy of the scribes, or the self-righteousness of the Pharisees, or the extortion of the lawyers, or his rejection by the nation he had come to save, while no voice could speak in words more fearful, yet none could speak in tones more tremulous with the deepest, tenderest emotion. But oh, how much more often the blessing breathed from his lip than the woe! Judgment was his strange work; mercy his delight. Truly in all his works, in all his ways, in all his discourses, the beautiful prophecy that foretold the gentleness of his grace was fulfilled: 'He shall come down like rain upon the mown grass: as showers that water the earth' (*Psa.* 72:6). 'A bruised reed shall he not break, and the smoking flax shall he not quench' (*Isa.* 42:3). But let us consider this specific illustration of Christ's gentleness – his dealings with the burdened. 'He gently leadeth those that are with young.'

We have an illustration of this in the considerate tenderness of Jacob: 'And he said unto him, My lord knoweth that the children are tender, and the flocks and herds with young are with me: and if men should overdrive them one day, all the flock will die. Let my lord, I pray thee, pass over before his servant: and I will lead on softly' (*Gen.* 33:13–14). If such the tenderness, such the consideration of man, what must be that of Christ! Who can portray the gentleness with which he leads his people? How great is his gentleness displayed in conversion! He draws them with cords of love and with the bands of a man – gradually unveiling their vileness and thus step by step leading them into assured peace. His teaching, how gentle! 'I have yet many things to say unto you, but ye cannot bear them now' (*John* 16:12). Here a little and there a little, he, by the Spirit, softly leads us to truth, doctrine explaining doctrine, precept leading to precept, promise following promise, and so, by a gradual unfolding of the gospel, by a process of instruction the most gentle, we are fed, first with the milk, and then with the strong meat of the Word, and so grow up into Christ, the Truth. Submit yourself, then, beloved, to his teaching. Burdened with a sense of your ignorance, wearied with the teaching of men, perplexed and discouraged by the conflicting of human judgment, come and learn of Christ. You will advance more in divine instruction in one day at the feet of Jesus than in a lifetime at the feet of Gamaliel. The very gentleness of his teaching instructs. His patience, forbearance, and painstaking, his words of heart-cheer and commendation untinged by an unkind look and untinctured by a harsh word, will advance your experimental knowledge of himself, and so advance your soul heavenward.

Not less gentle is his guidance. Is the path our heavenly Father has chosen for us paved with flint and sown with briar? Is it narrow and serpentine, difficult and perilous, often lone and dreary? How gently the Shepherd leads us along! How he goes before, straightening the crooked, and smoothing the rough places, and rolling the stone from before us! What unexpected mercies and interpositions and aids he causes to spring forth in our way; how he mitigates expected suffering, allays foreboding fears, and disappoints all our unbelieving and mournful anticipations, preventing us with his goodness! And when we have reached that event in our life which we dreaded most, the spot which looked the

darkest in our history, behold, we have stood amazed at
the marvellous loving-kindness of our God – that very
event has proved our greatest blessing, and that very
spot the sunniest and the brightest in the wilderness – so
gently has Jesus led us!

In affliction and sorrow, how gentle his dealings! Perhaps it is then that we learn more of this perfection of
our dear Lord than at any other time. The time of trial is
a time that tests the reality of things. It brings to the
proof the friendship of the world, the real help of the
creature, the actual sufficiency of all earthly things.
Times of affliction are truly times of trial. But the greatest
and grandest discovery of all is the sufficiency, the preciousness, and the gentleness of Christ. Oh, how little is
known of the 'Man of sorrows' but in the hour of sorrow! There are soundings in the depths of his infinite
love, tenderness, and sympathy only made in the many
and deep waters of adversity. How gently does he deal
with our burdened hearts then! There is not a being in
the universe that knows how to deal with sorrow, how
to heal a wounded spirit, how to bind up a broken heart,
as Jesus. Lord, teach us this truth. Lead us into the
depths of thy love. Unveil the springs of thy sympathy.
Shew us that in the languor of sickness, in the tortures of
pain, in the agony of bereavement, in the woundings of
trial, in the losses of adversity, thou still art gentle and
that thy gentleness maketh us great.

We need as much the gentleness of Christ in the
smooth as in the rough path. Smooth paths are slippery
paths. Times of prosperity are perilous times to the
Christian. Never is the man of God, the man of Christian
principle, more exposed to the corruption of his own nature, the assaults of Satan, and the deductions of the

world, as when the world prospers with him and the creature smiles upon him. Then is he walking upon enchanted ground, then he needs to pray, 'Hold thou me up, and I shall be safe' (*Psa.* 119:117). 'Let integrity and uprightness preserve me' (*Psa.* 25:21). Oh to be kept from this sinful, ungodly, treacherous world! If riches increase, to give the more to Christ; if honours accumulate, to walk the humbler with God; if influence and position and power augment, to write upon it all, 'HOLINESS UNTO THE LORD.' But what can thus preserve, thus sanctify, but the gentleness of Christ, who will not suffer the moon to smite us by night, nor the sun by day (*Psa.* 121:6), who, in the night-season of adversity and in the daytime of prosperity, hides us in the cleft of the rock and thus gently leads us heavenward?

And now, beloved, what a help heavenward, what strength and heart-cheer, will you find in a believing reception of this truth – the gentleness of Christ! Never doubt, never question, never reject it. It is an ingredient in every cup you drink, it is light in every cloud you behold, it is an accent in every voice you hear of Christ's dealings, leadings, and teachings. He is, he must be, gentle. He is not only gentle, but he is gentleness. Gentleness is his nature, because love is his essence. The heart of Christ is such that it cannot be otherwise than gentle in its every feeling. The physician is not less kind because he prescribes a nauseous remedy, nor the surgeon less feeling because he makes a deep incision, nor the parent less loving because he employs the rod. Nor is your Lord less so, because the way by which he leads, and the discipline by which he sanctifies, and the method by which he instructs you, may for a moment veil the reality, light, and comfort of this truth, 'He gently leadeth those that are with young'. Did Jacob lead the flocks and herds with young gently and softly lest they should die? Oh, how much more gently and softly does our Jacob, our true Shepherd, lead us! 'He shall feed his flock like a shepherd: he shall gather the lambs with his arm, and carry them in his bosom, and shall gently lead those that are with young.' Lest we should be weary, he will not overdrive us; lest we should faint, he leads us by springs of water; lest our soul should be discouraged by reason of the way, he causes us to lie down beneath the shadow of the Rock that is higher than we.

If this be so, then yield yourself to the Lord's leading. Be satisfied that he is leading you by the right way homeward. Do not distrust his wisdom, nor question his love, nor fret, murmur, and rebel that the way is not exactly just as you would have chosen. Be sure of this, it is the right way; and if it is one of self-denial and of difficulty, one of straitness and of cloud, yet it is the way home, the ordained way, the only way that will bring you into the beatific presence of Jesus. And his gentleness will constrain him to bear with you and will suggest just such wise and holy discipline as will impart robustness to your religion, completeness to your Christian character, and sanctity to all the relations and doings of life.

O Lord, I am oppressed, undertake for me; I am burdened, gently lead me; I am in darkness, stay my soul upon thee; I am in perplexity, skilfully guide me. Let me hear thy voice saying, 'This is the way, walk ye in it' (*Isa.* 30:21). Let thy pillar of cloud by day and of fire by night lead and guide me gently homeward. Make thy way straight before my feet. My foes watch for my halting, my enemies wait for my stumbling – hold thou me up, and I shall be safe. Sorrow swells my heart, tears dim my eyes, the billows swell, the sky lowers, the cloud darkens, the winds sigh mournfully, and all my landscape is wintry and cheerless – draw me within thy warm, thy sheltering love. Thou hast laid me upon this bed of weakness and of pain – come and make it in my sickness, and pillow this sleepless, weary head upon thy breast. Thou hast nipped my favorite flower, hast withered my pleasant gourd, hast removed my strong stay, hast dried up my present resources, and hast left me to tread the vale of life in loneliness, in want, and in tears – soothe, succour, and uphold my trembling heart, my weak faith, my desponding mind. 'In the multitude of my thoughts within me [let] thy comforts delight my soul' (*Psa.* 94:19). In my widowhood, in my orphanage, in my friendlessness, in my desolateness, in my need, I look, I run, I cleave to thee. Cast me not off from the bosom to which I fly. Shelter me from the storm and tempest within thy wounded side. Let that eye that never wanders in its glance of love, that voice that never falters in its accents of tenderness, that hand that never droops in its outstretched help, that heart that never chills, that faithfulness that never veers, restore, soothe, and engirdle me. Lord, no parent, no brother, no friend, no lover is like thee; and I am learning thy worth, thy gentleness, and thy preciousness in thine own appointed, wise, and holy way. Only let the result of this thy present dealing be my deeper holiness, my richer experience, my maturer Christianity, my greater usefulness, my more advanced meetness for heaven, my more simple, single, unreserved consecration to thee, and thy more undivided, undisputed, and supreme enthronement within my soul.

Is there a thing beneath the sun
  That strives with thee my heart to share?
Oh! tear it thence, and reign alone,
  The Lord of every motion there!

I cite you, my Christian hearer, as Christ's witness to this truth. Has not the Lord dealt gently with you? Gently has he carried you over the rough place, gently has he led you through the swelling tide, gently has he wounded, and with what gentleness has he healed you, gently has he chastened, and how gently has he dried your tears. With what gentleness has he dealt with you in sickness, in suffering, and in grief. How gently he has corrected your backslidings, restored your wanderings, guided your perplexities, removed your burdens; and thus, with a power that is never exhausted, with a skill that is never baffled, with a patience that never wearies, with a love that never falters, and with a gentleness that never overdrives, Christ is leading you step by step heavenward, where with a depth of gratitude and an emphasis of meaning unfelt before, you shall exclaim, 'Thy gentleness hath made me great' (2 *Sam.* 22:36, *Psa.* 18:35).

Beloved, burdened with sin, burdened with grief, burdened with sorrow, listen to the gentle voice which bids thee, 'Cast thy burden on the LORD, and he shall sustain thee' (*Psa.* 55:22). Thy burden, whatever it may be, thy burden of care, thy burden of anxiety, thy burden of sickness, thy burden of weariness, cast it upon Jesus the Burden-bearer, roll it from off thy shoulders upon his, transfer it from thy heart to his heart, in the simplicity and directness of a faith that doubts not, hesitates not, demurs not, because his word has promised that his grace and strength and love shall sustain you. No burden will Jesus have you feel but the easy burden of his commands, the gentle burden of his love, the honoured burden of his cross. In bearing these you shall find rest; for there is real rest in obedience, in love, in the cross, yea, in whatever binds the heart to Christ.

Imitate Christ in his gentleness. Be gentle to others as he is gentle to you. 'The servant of the Lord must not strive; but be gentle' (2 *Tim.* 2:24). The great apostle could say, 'We were gentle among you, even as a nurse cherisheth her children' (1 *Thess.* 2:7). 'The wisdom that is from above is first pure, then peaceable, gentle' (*James* 3:17), and it teaches us 'to speak evil of no man, to be no brawlers, but gentle, showing all meekness unto all men' (*Titus* 3:2). Be gentle to the lambs of the flock; be gentle to those whose grace is little, whose faith is weak, whose strength is small, whose infirmities are many, whose sorrows are keen, whose trials are severe, whose positions and paths in life are difficult and perilous. Oh, I beseech you, by the meekness and gentleness of Christ, that you be in this particular, Christ-like. Be gentle to them that have fallen by the power of temptation; those who have travelled in the ways of the Lord with so slow and tardy a step that they have been overtaken by evil. Be gentle to the bruised reed and the smoking flax. Be gentle, very gentle, to the broken heart and the wounded spirit. Speak gently to those whom shame and grief and sin have bowed down to the earth. Speak gently of those who, through weakness and frailty, have erred in judgment or in practice. Oh, learn of Jesus, in the gentleness with which he leads the burdened, and consider yourself as never so closely assimilated to him as when meekness, lowliness, and gentleness clothe you as with a garment, and beautify your whole carriage with their lustre.

Gently, Lord, oh, gently lead us
   Through this gloomy vale of tears,
Through the changes thou'st decreed us,
   Till our last great change appears.

When temptation's darts assail us,
   When in devious paths we stray,
Let thy goodness never fail us,
   Lead us in thy perfect way.

In the hour of pain and anguish,
   In the hour when death draws near,
Suffer not our hearts to languish,
   Suffer not our souls to fear.

When this mortal life is ended,
   Bid us in thine arms to rest,
Till, by angel bands attended,
   We awake among the blest.

Then, oh, crown us with thy blessing,
   Through the triumphs of thy grace;
Then shall praises never ceasing
   Echo through thy dwelling-place.

CHAPTER 4

The Clouds of the Christian, the Chariot of God

Who maketh the clouds his chariot.
— Psalm 104:3

If God were perfectly comprehensible in his being and government to a finite mind, then either he must forego his claim to divinity, or we must cease to be human. And yet in nothing, scarcely, is the Christian more at fault than in attempting to fathom those dispensations of his government in which he conceals his purposes and enshrouds himself; and failing, he then questions the wisdom and rectitude of his procedure! But how gently does the result rebuke and confound our misapprehension and distrust. When from the secret place of thunder he utters his voice, when in his dealings darkness is under his feet, when he makes darkness his secret place, his pavilion round about him dark waters and thick clouds of the skies (*Psa.* 18:11), even then he is but making a way for his love to us, which shall appear all the more real and precious by the very cloud-chariot in which it travels. The believer in Christ has nothing slavishly to dread, but everything filially to hope from God. So fully is he pardoned, so completely is he justified, so perfectly is he reconciled to God, that even the darkest dispensations in which he hides himself shall presently unveil the brightest views of his character and love; and thus the lowering cloud that deepened in its darkness and grew larger as it approached shall dissolve and vanish, leaving no object visible to the eye but him whose essence and name is love. Oh, it is because we have such shallow views of God's love that we have such defective views of God's dealings! We blindly interpret the symbols of his providence because we so imperfectly read the engraving of his heart. Faith finds it difficult to spell the word 'love' as written in the shaded characters of its discipline; to believe that the cloud which looks so sombre and threatening is the love-chariot of him who for our ransom gave himself unto the death because he so loved us!

The subject on which this chapter engages our thoughts presents another path heavenward for the Christian. And as this path is frequently trodden by many, we desire to present it in such an aspect as shall help onward those who are walking in darkness having no light, or around whose way the dense dark clouds of divine dispensations are gathering, filling the soul with fear and trembling. He makes the clouds his chariot; and soothed with this assurance, the beclouded, benighted traveller may be still and know that he is God. Let us view some of those clouds of the Christian pilgrimage which Christ makes his chariot.

The heavens are draped with many clouds of varied forms and hues. Such are, figuratively, the dealings of God with his people. Our Lord has many chariots. It is recorded of Solomon that his chariots were fourteen hundred; but the chariots of God are twenty thousand. In every cloud in the history of the church and in the experience of the saints is a divine chariot, and every chariot is, like the King of Israel's, paved in the midst with love. We may illustrate this by a reference to Christ's state-chariot, or, in other words, the Lord's appearance to his people in the cloud of his essential and divine glory. It was in this cloud he entered and filled the tabernacle 'so that the priests could not stand to minister because of the cloud: for the glory of the LORD filled the house of the LORD' (*1 Kings* 8:11). In this same cloud, too, he descended upon Mount Sinai: 'And a cloud covered the mount. And the glory of the LORD abode upon mount Sinai' (*Exod.* 24:15–16). The same glorious chariot was seen descending and lighting upon Mount Tabor, in that sublime and expressive scene of our Lord's transfiguration, when 'he received from God the Father honour and glory, when there came such a voice to him from the excellent glory, This is my beloved Son, in whom I am well pleased' (*2 Pet.* 1:17). The same chariot of state waited his ascension and bore him back to heaven, reinvested with the glory which he had with the Father before the world was; for as he went up and his form disappeared from the gaze of his disciples, 'a cloud received him out of their sight' (*Acts* 1:9). In like manner, descending in the state-chariot of his own glory and the glory of his Father, shall he come again. 'Behold, he cometh with clouds; and every eye shall see him' (*Rev.* 1:7). Solemn scene! Sublime advent! Blessed hope of those who love and look and long for his appearing! Saints of God, it speedeth on! The day of your full redemption draweth nigh. The state-chariot of our Immanuel is preparing for its descent to the world, conveying him to his church, his loving, longing bride. Lord, why tarry the wheels of thy chariot? Come, quickly come, and terminate the reign of sin and sorrow and death in the dominion of holiness and happiness and endless life, and take thy wearying church to thyself.

> Come, great Redeemer, open wide
>   The curtains of the parting sky;
> On a bright cloud in triumph ride,
>   And on the wind's swift pinions fly.
>
> Come, King of kings, with thy bright train,
>   Cherubs and seraphs, heavenly hosts;
> Assume thy right, enlarge thy reign,
>   As far as earth extends her coasts.
>
> Come, Lord, and where thy cross once stood,
>   There plant thy banner, fix thy throne;
> Subdue the rebels by thy Word,
>   And claim the nations as thine own.

May we not pause at this part of our subject and ask the reader, have you seen the King riding in his chariot of state? To drop the figure, have you seen his glory, as the glory of the only-begotten of the Father, full of grace and truth? Oh, it is a grand spectacle, the glory that is in Christ Jesus, the glory of his person, his atoning work, his redeemed church! Blessed are the eyes enlightened to behold it! Deem not your Christianity as true, nor your religion as sound, nor your hope as valid, unless you have seen by faith's spiritual, far-discerning eye Jesus in his divinity, the King riding in majesty and beauty in this cloud-chariot of his essential dignity and glory. It is only in the beaming effulgence of this glory that all our demerit and deformity is absorbed and annihilated. So divine, blinding, and overpowering is the essential glory of our redeeming God that a believing sinner, enveloped by its beams, is changed into the same image, from glory to glory, even as by the Spirit of the Lord. All his unrighteousness, his sins, and hell-deservings are consumed and destroyed by the divine Sun of righteousness. Jesus makes this cloud his chariot and waits to bless us with its vision.

There are, too, divine truths – the mysteries of the gospel, for example – which may be regarded as the cloud-chariots of God. It is a favourite maxim with the objector to Christianity – plausible yet fallacious – that where mystery begins faith terminates. And yet never did the genius of error forge a weapon more weak and powerless with which to attack our divine and holy faith! If the Bible be the revelation of God, mysteries must necessarily form an essential part, if not its very substance. It would indeed be astonishing if God should not know more than man; or that if, in condescending to reveal to man his being, his will, and his heart, there should not be problems in divine truth man cannot solve, depths he cannot reach, mysteries he cannot unravel, and revelations he may not reconcile. Such, for example, are the revealed doctrines of the Trinity, the incarnation, atonement, election, sovereignty, the new birth, and resurrection. We own the mystery which envelops so much connected with these great verities of our faith; that there are depths too profound for reason's line to touch, modes of existence which forbid the rash doubts of the sceptic and the vain speculation of the philosopher, while they demand the unquestioning faith and profound homage of the believing mind.

And yet are we then to reject them? We may, we do, believe a thousand things in nature which the mind cannot fully comprehend. Our very existence is a mystery; every movement of the body, every action of mind, every volition of will, every emotion and affection of the heart encompasses us with mystery. Yet on that account do we doubt our own existence? My being confounds, but does it transcend my reason? And are we not at every step confronting mysteries in nature and in providence which we accept as credible, which otherwise we must reject as incomprehensible? If, then, my reader, your mind is perplexed, agitated, and distressed respecting these clouds which veil so much connected with the revealed truths of the gospel, learn this lesson – that Christ makes these very clouds his chariot. In each and all of these profound yet glorious verities of our faith, these great and precious doctrines of the gospel, Christ is revealed, Christ is embodied, Christ travels. The gospel is the vehicle in which Christ makes his constant advent to our souls; and if our reason may not be able perfectly to comprehend all the parts of the vehicle, let it content our faith that Jesus, the revelation, the substance, and glory of all divine truth, occupies it; and that ere long the cloud of mystery into which we entered with trembling will, as in the transfiguration, dissolve into light and splendour, pure and soothing, and we shall see Jesus only.

Regard it as one of your chief mercies that your salvation depends not upon reason but upon faith. You are not called upon fully to comprehend, but unquestioningly to believe and love. You are not the less saved because your faith deals with obscurity, nor is your faith less real, precious, or saving because it abjures the wisdom of the sage for the docile spirit of the child, and the learning of the philosopher for the humility of the disci-

ple. Let your great study be the mystery of Christ's love
to sinners – the mystery of Christ's love to you. The
apostle was content to leave all mysteries to the day of
perfect knowledge, if he could but attain unto love.
Though I know all mysteries, and have not love, I am
nothing. Study that grand truth, 'God is love', as embodied in the cross of Christ, and you can well afford to refer
all that is obscure and hard to understand in revealed
truth to the day when we shall know all, as we also are
known. Cease to dispute, cavil, and speculate on the subject of religion and revealed truth, and receive the gospel
and enter into the kingdom of Christ as a little child.

In the momentous matter of your future destiny, you
have but to deal with two specific and distinct facts –
your sinnership and Christ's Saviourship. What if you
solve all the problems of science, and fathom all the
depths of learning, and unravel all the mysteries of
truth, and yet are lost! What will your speculations, and
researches, and discoveries avail, if at last they be found
ineffectual to distil one drop of the water of life upon the
tongue, now cavilling and profane, then fevered and
tormented in the quenchless flame? Are you not, by
your present persistent course of unbelief, pride, and rejection of truth, in danger of finding yourself there? Oh,
it is of infinite importance to you that you come as sinful
to the blood of Christ, as condemned to his righteousness, as ignorant and unlearned to the feet of Christ. The
great problem you have to work out is your own salvation. The grand mystery you have to unravel is the
mystery of your union with Jesus. The momentous questions you have to decide are the place, the society, and
the employments of your endless future! Where, with
whom, and how will you spend your long eternity?

Compared with these grave considerations, all your doctrinal hair-splitting and your religious speculations, your vain disputes and your dreamy hopes, are as the follies of drivelling idiocy, or the aberrations of a mind insane.

Shakespeare portrays his 'Lear' as gathering straws with the hand that had wielded a sceptre, and devoting to childish thoughts a mind which once gave laws to a kingdom. With a yet more powerful hand the sacred historian describes the monarch of Babylon quitting the occupation and abodes of men and betaking himself to the pursuits and companionship of irrational animals. But what are these sad pictures of a mind diseased, wrecked, and ruined, compared with the moral madness of the man who disbelieves the gospel, cavils at truth, and perils the eternal interests of his soul – who employs the rational powers with which God has endowed him in attempting to subvert the foundations of Christianity, to extinguish the beacon light erected on the headlands and the shores of time to guide the spiritual voyager safe to eternity, involving in the destruction of others his own personal salvation?

The clouds of God's providential government are no less his chariot. 'Clouds and darkness are round about him' (*Psa.* 97:2), and in these dispensations of his government he moves among men, and especially his saints. It is by a 'cloudy pillar', sometimes turning towards us gleams of light, at other times casting deep and dark shadows on our way, that God is conducting us heavenward. Oh, how many and how varied in form and in hue are the trying, afflictive, and disciplinary dealings of our heavenly Father! How soon the bright blue sky smiling down upon us may be wreathed with the drapery of clouds, each one dark and portentous. God blows upon wealth and it vanishes, touches health and it droops, smites the creature and it dies, and we exclaim in the words of David, 'I am weary with my groaning; all the night make I my bed to swim; I water my couch with my tears' (*Psa.* 6:6). But the night of cloud and gloom is to the kingdom of grace what the darkness of night is to the kingdom of nature. Darkness possesses the twofold property of concealing and revealing; and it would perhaps be impossible to say in which it most excelled, whether it does not reveal as much, if not more, beauty and wonder than it veils. Those clouds of providential dispensations which turn our day into night bring out to view such constellations of divine promises, discover such perfections of the divine character, and present such discoveries of divine love, as to make even night more wonderful and resplendent than day. Ah, beloved, we should know but little what Christ's chariot of love was, but for the clouds in which he comes to us! Are cloudy dispensations gathering around you? Are God's ways such as fill you with fear and foreboding, agitation and alarm? Does sickness threaten, do resources fail, friendships chill, changes in the relations or social position of life approach? Is separation feared, death anticipated, followed in its gloomy wake by weakened dependencies, closed channels, sundered ties, the sad farewell to a parent's society, the home of childhood, and the dearest, sweetest ties of earth? Oh, these gathering clouds are but the Lord's chariot, in which he rides to thee in all the wisdom of his dealings, the faithfulness of his covenant, the tenderness of his love, and the righteousness of his procedure.

> *Ye fearful saints, fresh courage take;*
> *The clouds ye so much dread*
> *Are big with mercy, and shall break*
> *In blessings on your head.*

Judge not the Lord by feeble sense,
  But trust him for his grace;
  Behind a frowning providence
  He hides a smiling face.

But consider *who* it is that rides in this chariot. It is the Lord your God. Many of God's people are so absorbed in their contemplation of the chariot as to overlook the one who sits in it. Their emotions vary according to the appearance which it presents. If the cloud is bright and promising, their feelings and hopes are correspondingly so; but should it wear a sombre, threatening appearance, faith sinks and fears rise. But faith has nothing to do with the chariot, whatever may be its magnitude, shape, or hue, but with Christ in the chariot and with God in the cloud. For example, with regard to divine truth, it is not with the vehicle of truth itself, but with Christ as revealed in the truth, that our faith must deal. I may not be able to comprehend and understand all the parts of the chariot – its complexity may baffle, its gorgeousness may blind me – but I may be able to see and understand who is enthroned upon its seat.

If the mystery of the doctrine of the Trinity, and of the incarnation, and of the atonement, and of election, is so profound that I cannot explain or comprehend it, I still may discern in them one glorious object, and discerning that object, it were enough for my salvation. I can see Jesus in the Trinity, Jesus in the incarnation, Jesus in the atonement, Jesus in election, and this will suffice until the night of divine mysteries gives place to the meridian sunshine of a perfect and eternal day of knowledge and glory; and then I shall as fully understand the mysterious construction and comprehend all the different parts of the chariot as my mind will be capable of knowing, and my heart of loving him, whose name is Wonderful, who rode in it to my salvation. Then shall we know even as also we are known. Oh, how fully and blessedly shall we know Jesus then! How gloriously will this great mystery of godliness, God manifest in the flesh, unveil to our enlarged and sanctified intellect. We shall no more see the King in his beauty as through a glass darkly, nor the good land very far off. With souls perfected in holiness, how clear will be the vision, how transparent the medium, how glorious the Object! There shall be no more night of mystery, no more night of obscurity, no more night of sin, no more night of weeping. No disease shall shade the intellect, no prejudice shall warp, no shock shall unhinge it. No adversity shall touch the heart, no bereavement shall sadden, no changed and chilled affection shall collapse it.

That there will be *gradations* of knowledge and *degrees* of glory, I think is probable. There are so in the Church of God on earth; I see nothing to exclude the same from the Church of God in heaven. But this will not in the slightest degree affect the happiness or glory of the saints. Is there less beauty in a tulip-bed, or in a conservatory of flowers, because there is so rich an assemblage of varied colours? Or, is there less splendour in the heavenly bodies because there is so great a variety of magnitude, effulgence, and orbit? And will there be less enjoyment, or less beauty, or less song amidst the countless numbers who throng the temple above, because 'one star differeth from another star in glory' (*1 Cor.* 15:41)? Oh, no, the glory and the happiness of each will be full and perfect! Every spirit will possess a happiness and reflect a glory equal to its capacity. As two luminous bodies in the celestial system may shine in perfection, though in widely different orbits and with different degrees of splendour, and as two streams, the rivulet and the river, may course their way through landscape, the one gliding in simple, pensive beauty, the other rolling in majestic waves, and yet each filling its channel, both equally charming the eye and declaring the glory of God; so the 'spirits of just men made perfect' (*Heb.* 12:23) shall each be a differing, yet full, vessel of happiness. The image of God will shine with full-orbed splendour in both, though with different intensity, and by each one shall Christ perfect to himself endless praise.

Oh, beloved, if we but reach that world of purity and of bliss, we shall be so satisfied with the orbit we roll in, the glory we emit, and the happiness we feel, as never to question the goodness or the righteousness of God in the sphere assigned us! Christ will then be all in all to us, and we shall be satisfied with all that Christ has done. I think that our bliss will be so complete, our joy so full, and our glory so resplendent, we shall scarcely be conscious that there is another saint fuller, happier, or more glorious than ourselves. Blessed world of glory, we long to be within thy walls! Open, ye everlasting doors, and admit us, that we may eat of the tree of life and recline upon the sunlight banks of the crystal river that makes glad the city of our God.

> *Salem, city of the holy,*
>   *We shall be within thy walls:*
> *There, beside yon crystal river,*
>   *There, beneath life's wondrous tree,*
> *There, with nought to cloud or sever,*
>   *Ever with the Lamb to be!*
> *Heir of glory!*
>   *That shall be for thee and me!*

The Lord, too, is equally in all the providential clouds which unfold his government and trace our pilgrimage heavenward. It is our wisdom and our happiness to know that there is not an event or circumstance, a cloud or a sunbeam, in our personal history and experience that is not a vehicle of Christ. He makes the clouds his chariot; and his providential dispensations, whatever their form or their hue, are his means of approaching and visiting us. 'The LORD hath his way in the whirlwind and in the storm, and the clouds are the dust of his feet' (*Nahum* 1:3). Fear not, oh Christian traveller, that dark, lowering cloud rising above thee. It grows large, and it looks threatening, and thou thinkest it will overtake and consume thee before thou hast crossed the plain and reached the shelter. Tremble not, it will roll no thunder, it will flash no lightning! The cross of Christ is the great lightning conductor for the Church of God. Around that cross, law and justice met in awful array, the thunderbolt struck and the lightning scathed the Son of God, and upon him they spent their force. And now beneath the shelter of that cross, the penitent sinner may safely stand, and the darkest cloud, and the loudest thunder, and the most vivid lightning that gathers and verberates and illumines above shall pass him by untouched, for there is now 'no condemnation to them which are in Christ Jesus' (*Rom.* 8:1).

Why, then, fear the dealings, and the leadings, and the chastenings of God in providence? That sombre chariot that appears at thy door, enters thy abode, mounts into thy chamber, is the chariot of love, the chariot of Jesus. Christ is in that adversity, Christ is in that loss, Christ is in that bereavement, Christ is in that sickness; in a word, that cloud, whatever may be its nature, its form, and its darkness what it may, is one of the twenty thousand chariots of God in which he rideth to thy help, in his excellency, on the sky. Oh, learn to see Christ and to deal closely with God in all his dispensations and dealings with you. No enemy bent on destruction, no foe armed with vengeance, sits in the cloud chariot that approaches you – it is your Father, your covenant God, your Redeemer. It is he to whose heart you are more precious than the universe, in whose eye you are more beautiful than angels, and on whose ear the accents of your voice fall with a melody infinitely surpassing the sweetest cherub before the throne.

Look not, I beseech you, at the sombre hue of the chariot, but rather at the love and loveliness and graciousness of him who sits within it. It is your beloved Lord! His person is white and ruddy, human and divine. His countenance is brighter than the sun shining in its strength. His voice is gentle, tender, and winning, uttering the speech and the accent and the words of love. Then be not afraid. Christ will never send an empty chariot to his people. When his chariot lights at our door, we may be assured that he is in it. No angel, no ransomed spirit shall occupy the seat, but he himself. Welcome, then, the visit of your gracious King. He comes laden with the 'sure mercies of David', freighted with covenant blessings and bearing the sweet grapes and the fragrant flowers gleaned from the vineyards and the paradise of heaven. He comes in this cloud to talk with and to manifest himself to you and to make you more intimately and personally acquainted with himself, with his truth and his love. Welcome him to your dwelling, receive him into your heart, and bid him abide with you there, never to leave you again. Be not satisfied unless you discern the King in the chariot. This only will dispel your fears and reconcile you to the dispensation, however dark and painful it may be. The moment you realize, 'Thou art near, O Lord' – that moment your heaving, panting bosom will be at rest. The disciples feared as they entered into the cloud upon the Mount of Transfiguration, but discovering the Lord in it, their trembling was changed into confidence, their apprehension into joy, and they desired to build their tabernacle on its summit and no more descend to the toil and the strife below.

Beloved, are you entering some overshadowing cloud trembling and apprehensive? Fear not! Thy Lord is in it, and a Father's voice of love shall speak to thee from out of its veiling shadows, saying, 'When thou passest through the waters, I will be with thee; and through the rivers, they shall not overflow thee: when thou walkest through the fire, thou shalt not be burned; neither shall the flame kindle upon thee. For I am the LORD thy God, the Holy One of Israel, thy Saviour' (*Isa.* 43:2–3). Glorious cloud that enshrines the form of my redeeming God! Welcome, thou coming chariot, that brings Jesus near to my soul. Thy vesture is dark, thy form gigantic, thy appearance threatening, but my heart shall not fear, nor my faith falter, for in this will I be confident, that he makes the clouds his chariot, and in this chariot comes my Saviour to shelter, to soothe, and to bless me. Truly, 'there is none like unto the God of Jeshurun, who rideth upon the heaven in thy help, and in his excellency on the sky. The eternal God is thy refuge, and underneath are the everlasting arms' (*Deut.* 33:26–27).

Ere long another chariot will appear at your door, the chariot sent to bear you home to God, to Christ, to heaven. We know not what form this messenger will assume, whether it will be Christ's state-chariot, which shall convey him in person to us, or whether it shall be Christ's chariot of death, which will convey us to him; but this we believe and are assured of, that in a very little while we shall see the Lord and be with him forever. The chariot is preparing for us, let us be preparing for the chariot. Let us so live detached from, and above, the world, and creatures, and earthly delights; let us so live in fellowship with God and in communion with divine and eternal things, that when the Lord's chariot gently knocks at our door, we may have nothing to do but to step into it and away to heaven! Aged saint, art thou looking through the window and the lattice of thy frail tabernacle, exclaiming, 'Why is his chariot so long in coming? why tarry the wheels of his chariots?' (*Judg.* 5:28).

Be patient and trustful; the Lord's time is best, and ere long thou shalt exclaim, 'It is the voice of my Beloved that knocketh! The Master is come and calleth for me. Earth, farewell! Friends, farewell! Parents, kindred, wife, children, home, farewell! Sorrow, suffering, trial, sin, farewell! I go to be with Jesus forever!' And then a cloud of glory shall receive you out of their sight, and so shall you ever be with the Lord.

> *Forever with the Lord!*
> *Amen; so let it be;*
> *Life from the dead is in that word,*
> *'Tis immortality.*

> *Here in the body pent,*
> *Absent from him I roam,*
> *Yet nightly pitch my moving tent*
> *A day's march nearer home.*

My Father's house on high,
Home of my soul, so near,
At times, to faith's far-seeing eye
Thy golden gates appear!

Yet clouds will intervene,
And all my prospect flies,
Like Noah's dove, I flit between
Rough seas and stormy skies.

Anon the clouds depart,
The winds and waters cease,
While sweetly o'er my gladden'd heart
Expands the bow of peace.

In darkness as in light,
Hidden alike from view,
I sleep, I wake, as in his sight,
Who looks all nature through.

Forever with the Lord!
Father, if 'tis thy will,
The promise of that faithful word
Even here to me fulfil.

Be thou at my right hand,
Then can I never fail;
Uphold thou me, and I shall stand,
Fight, and I must prevail.

Knowing as I am known,
How shall I love that word!
And oft repeat before the throne,
Forever with the Lord!

Forever with the Lord!
Amen; so let it be;
Life from the dead is in that word,
'Tis immortality.

CHAPTER 5

Trial, a Help Heavenward

That we must through much tribulation enter into the kingdom of God.

— Acts 14:22

There are few things in the spiritual history of the child of God more really helpful heavenward than sanctified trial. He treads no path in which he finds aids more favourable to advancement in the divine life, circumstances which contribute more to the development and completeness of Christian character – the teaching, the quickening, the purifying – than the path of hallowed sorrow; sorrow which a covenant God has sent, which grace sanctifies, and which knits the heart to Christ. The atmosphere is not more purified by the electric storm, nor the earth more fructified by the descending rain, than is the regenerate soul advanced in its highest interests by the afflictive dealings in God's government of his saints. 'Sweet are the uses of adversity' to an heir of heaven. Its form may appear 'ugly and venomous', for 'no chastening for the present seemeth to be joyous, but grievous'; nevertheless it 'bears a precious jewel in its head', for 'afterward it yieldeth the peaceable fruit of righteousness unto them which are exercised thereby' (*Heb.* 12:11). Affliction is to the believer what the wing is to the lark and what the eye is to the eagle, the means by which the soul mounts in praise heavenward, gazing closely and steadily upon the glorious Sun of righteousness. Chastening seals our sonship, sorrow disciplines the heart, affliction propels the soul onward. We should have a more vivid conception of the power of affliction as an ingredient of holiness if we kept more constantly in remembrance the fact that all the afflictive, trying dispensations of the believer are covenant dispensations, that they are not of the same character nor do they produce the same results as in the ungodly. They are among the 'sure mercies of David'. In the case of the unregenerate, all afflictions are a part and parcel of the curse and work naturally against their good; but in the case of the regenerate, they are, in virtue of the covenant of grace, transformed into blessings and work spiritually for their good. Just as the mountain stream coursing its way meets some sanative mineral by which it becomes endowed with a healing property, so afflictions, passing through the covenant, change their character, derive a sanctifying property, and thus become a healing medicine to the soul.

Thus we find tribulation the ancient and beaten path of the Church of God. A great cloud of witnesses all testify to sorrow as the ordained path to heaven. Both Christ and his apostles gently forewarned the saints that 'in the world ye shall have tribulation' (*John* 16:33), and that 'we must through much tribulation enter into the kingdom of God' (*Acts* 14:22). Here may be descried the trail of the flock and, yet more deeply and visibly imprinted, the footsteps of the Great Shepherd of the sheep, 'leaving us an example, that ye should follow his steps' (*1 Pet.* 2:21). Who, then, with Christ in his heart, the hope of glory, would wish exemption from what is common to the whole Church of God? Who would not sail to glory in the same vessel with Jesus and his disciples, tossed though that vessel be amidst the surging waves of life's troubled ocean? All shall arrive in heaven at last, 'some on boards, and some on broken pieces of the ship...[but] all safe to land' (*Acts* 27:44). It is not necessary, beloved reader, that in a chapter devoted to an exposition of the blessings which flow from sanctified trial, we enumerate all, or even any, of the varied forms which trial assumes. The truth with which we have now to do is the impetus that trial gives to the soul heavenward – the friendly hand it outstretches to assist the Christian pilgrim to his shrine, the traveller to his journey's end, the child to his Father's house.

Our first remark, then, with regard to trial, is that it is a time of spiritual instruction and so a help heavenward. It is not blindly but intelligently that we walk in the ways of the Lord and are travelling home to God. Great stress is laid by the Holy Ghost in the writings of the apostle upon the believer's advance in spiritual knowledge. In his prayer for the Ephesian saints he asks for them, that 'the God of our Lord Jesus Christ, the Father of glory, may give unto you the spirit of wisdom and revelation in the knowledge of him: the eyes of your understanding being enlightened' (*Eph.* 1:17–18). In another place he exhorts the saints to 'grow in grace, and in the knowledge of our Lord and Saviour Jesus Christ' (2 *Pet.* 3:18). In his own personal experience he set no limit to his spiritual knowledge: 'that I might know Christ' was the great aspiration of his soul, and he counted all things but loss for the excellency of the knowledge of Christ Jesus his Lord.

Now, the school of trial is the school of spiritual knowledge. We grow in a knowledge of ourselves, learning more of our superficial attainments, shallow experience, and limited grace. We learn, too, more of our weakness, emptiness, and vileness, the ploughshare of trial penetrating deep into the heart and throwing up its veiled iniquity. And oh, how does this deeper self-knowledge lay us low, humble and abase us; and when our self-sufficiency and our self-seeking and our self-glorying is thus mowed down, then the showers of the Saviour's grace descend 'as rain upon the mown grass', and so we advance in knowledge and holiness heavenward. We know more of the Lord Jesus through one sanctified affliction than by all the treatises the human pen ever wrote. Christ is only savingly known as he is known personally and experimentally. Books cannot teach him, sermons cannot teach him, lectures cannot teach him; they may aid our information and correct our views, but to know him as he is and as we ought, we must have personal dealings with him. Our sins must bring us to his blood, our condemnation must bring us to his righteousness, our corruptions must bring us to his grace, our wants must bring us to his fulness, our weakness must bring us to his strength, our sorrow must bring us to his sympathy, and his own loveliness and love must attract us to himself. And oh, in one hour, in a single transaction, in a lone sorrow, which has brought us to Jesus, who can estimate how rapidly and to what an extent we have grown in a knowledge of his person and work, his character and love?

I need not enlarge upon other branches of spiritual knowledge which trial promotes – how it increases our personal intimacy with God as our loving Father and

Friend; and how it opens our understanding to discern the deep things of God in the Scriptures, so that the Bible in the hour of affliction appears like a new revelation to us. Oh yes, times of trial are times of growth in experimental knowledge. We see God and Jesus and truth from new stand-points and in a different light, and we thank the Lord for the storm which dispelled the mist that hid all this glory, unveiling so lovely a landscape and so serene a sky to our view. Beloved, is the Lord now bringing your religion to the touchstone of trial, testing your experience and knowledge and faith in the crucible? Be calm in the assurance that he but designs your advancement in an experimental acquaintance with himself and his gospel, and that you shall emerge from it testifying, 'I have seen more of my own vileness, have known more of Jesus, have penetrated deeper into the heart of God, have a clearer understanding of revealed truth, and have learned more of the mysteries of the divine life, on this bed of sickness, in this time of bereaved sorrow, in this dark cloud that has overshadowed me, than in all my life before.' 'Blessed is the man whom thou chastenest, O LORD, and teachest him out of thy law' (*Psa.* 94:12). Oh yes, we learn God's power to support, his wisdom to guide, his love to comfort us, in a degree we could not have learned but in the way of trial.

Trial quickens us in prayer, and so effectually helps us heavenward. The life of God in the soul on earth is a life of communion of the soul with God in heaven. Prayer is nothing less than the divine nature in fellowship with the divine, the renewed creature in communion with God. And it would be as impossible for a regenerate soul to live without prayer, as for the natural life to exist without breathing. Oh, what a sacred and precious privilege is this! Is there one to be compared with it? When we have closed the door – for we speak now of that most solemn and holy habit of prayer, private communion – and have shut out the world, and the creature, and even the saints, and are closeted in personal, solemn, and confiding audience with God, what words can portray the preciousness and solemnity of that hour! Then is guilt confessed, and backslidings deplored, and care unburdened, and sorrow unveiled, and pardon sought, and grace implored, and blessings invoked, in all the filial trustfulness of a child unbosoming itself in the very depths of a father's love, pity, and succour.

But precious and costly as is this privilege of prayer, we need rousing to its observance. Trial is eminently instrumental in this. God often sends affliction for the accomplishment of this one end, that we might be stirred up to take hold of him. 'LORD, in trouble have they visited thee, they poured out a prayer when thy chastening was upon them' (*Isa.* 26:16). To whom in sorrow do we turn, to whom in difficulty do we repair, to whom in need do we fly but to the Lord? If in prosperity we have 'waxed fat and kicked', if when the sun has shone upon us we have walked independently and proudly and distantly, now that affliction has overtaken us we are humbled and prostrate at his feet; retrace our steps, return to God, and find a new impulse given to, and a new power and meetness and soothing in, communion with God. Be assured of this, my reader, there is no help heavenward like unto prayer. There is no ladder the rungs of which will bring you so near to God, there are no wings the plumage of which will carry you so close to heaven as prayer. The moment you have unpinioned your soul for communion with God, let your

pressure, your sorrow, your sin be what it may, that moment your heart has departed earth and is on its way
heavenward. You are soaring above the region of sorrow
and battle and sin, and your spirit is expatiating beneath
a purer, happier, sunnier sky. Oh the soothing, the
strengthening, the uplifting found in prayer beneath the
cross! Thus trial helps us heavenward by quickening us
to devotion, by stirring us up to closeness of walk.

Child of God, do you desire speedier advance heavenward? Seek it in closer converse with God. Oh, what
mighty power has prayer! It has controlled the elements
of nature, stopped the sun in its course, and stayed the
arm of God. A man mighty in the prayer of faith is
clothed with an invincible panoply. He is in possession
of a force which Omnipotence cannot resist, for he has
power with God and prevails. Oh, turn your difficulty
into prayer, turn your sorrow into prayer, turn your want
into prayer, turn your very sins and backslidings into confession, supplication, and prayer, and on its wing your
soul shall rise to a region of thought and feeling and fellowship close to the very gates of heaven! Lord, we thank
thee for the sacred privilege of prayer; we thank thee for
the mercy-seat, sprinkled with blood, the place of prayer;
we thank thee for Jesus' precious name, our only plea in
prayer; we thank thee for the divine grace of prayer, and
not less, Lord, do we praise thee for the trial, the suffering, the sorrow which stimulates our languid spirit and
wakes our dormant heart to the holy, earnest exercise of
prayer!

Trials are necessary to wean us from the world. Perhaps nothing possesses so detaching, divorcing an effect
in the experience of the Christian as affliction. The world
is a great snare to the child of God. Its rank is a snare, its

possessions are a snare, its honours are a snare, its enter-
prises are a snare, the very duties and engagements of
daily life are a snare, to a soul whose citizenship is in
heaven and whose heart yearns to be more frequently
and exclusively where Jesus, its treasure, is. Oh, how the
things that are seen veil the things that are not seen!
How do things temporal banish from our thoughts and
affections and desires the things that are eternal! Why
does the sun appear so small an orb, so minute a speck
to our eye? Simply because of its remote distance. Oh, is
it not thus that Christ with his surpassing loveliness, and
heaven with its winning attractions, and eternal things
with their profound solemnity, and communion with
God in Christ, so soothing and precious, are objects so
dim and superficial just because we of the earth earthy,
live at so great a distance from God and allow the influence of the world an ascendancy over us so supreme
and absorbing? But God in wisdom and mercy sends us
trial to detach us from earth, to lessen our worldly mind-
edness, more deeply to convince us how empty and
insufficient is all created good when his chastening is
upon us, to intensify our affection for spiritual things,
and to bring our souls nearer to himself. 'Take away the
dross from the silver, and there shall come forth a vessel
for the finer' (*Prov.* 25:4). 'I will turn my hand upon thee,
and purely purge away thy dross, and take away all thy
tin' (*Isa.* 1:25).

Oh, when the heart is chastened and subdued by
sorrow, when the soul is smitten and humbled by adversity, when death bereaves, or sickness invades, or
resources narrow, or calamity in one of its many crushing forms lights heavily upon us, how solemn, earnest,
and distinct is the voice of our ascended Redeemer, 'If ye

be risen with me, seek those things which are above,
where I sit at the right hand of God. Set your affections
on things above, not on things on the earth. I am your
Treasure, your Portion, your All. Sharers of my
resurrection-life, you are partakers of its holy, quickening power and its heaven-bestowing blessings. Soon to
be with me in glory, let your heart travel thitherward,
and in its loosenings from earth, its divorcements from
the creature, cultivate the mind of my holy apostle, who
desired to depart and be with me.' Oh that to this touching appeal our hearts may respond, 'Lord, whom have I
in heaven but thee? and there is none upon earth that I
desire beside thee. Thou hast stricken and wounded and
laid me low, but thou wilt comfort, heal, and raise me up
again. Righteous art thou, O Lord, when I plead with
thee; yet let me talk with thee of thy judgments. Let this
trial detach me from the world, wean me from my idols,
transfer my heart to thee, and speed my soul with a
quicker step heavenward.' Thus the heart, crusted by
the continuous influence of earthly things, is mellowed
by sorrow through the sanctifying power of the Holy
Ghost. Then the Word becomes more fruitful, and the
Lord Jesus grows more precious and conformity to God
more promoted, earth recedes and heaven approaches,
and we exclaim in the words of the psalmist, 'Before I
was afflicted I went astray: but now have I kept thy
word' (*Psa.* 119:67). 'It is good for me that I have been afflicted; that I might learn thy statutes' (*Psa.* 119:71).

Thus, as an old divine wrote,

Afflictions are God's most effectual means to keep us
from losing our way to our heavenly rest. Without this
hedge of thorns on the right hand and on the left, we
should hardly keep the way to heaven. If there be but

one gap open, how ready are we to find it and turn out at it! When we grow wanton, or worldly, or proud, how doth sickness or other afflictions reduce us! Every Christian, as well as Luther, can call affliction one of his best schoolmasters; and with David may say, 'Before I was afflicted I went astray: but now have I kept thy word.' Many thousand rescued sinners may cry, O healthful sickness! O comfortable sorrow! O gainful losses! O enriching poverty! O blessed day that ever I was afflicted! Not only the green pastures and still waters, but the rod and staff, they comfort us. Though the Word and the Spirit do the main work, yet suffering so unbolts the door of the heart, that the Word hath easier entrance.

The moral purity of heart which chastened trial produces must have a distinct and prominent place in this enumeration of helps heavenward. Holiness, as it is an essential element of heaven, becomes an essential element in our spiritual meetness for its enjoyment. The inspired declaration is as solemn as it is emphatic, 'Holiness, without which no man shall see the Lord' (*Heb.* 12:14). The beautiful beatitude of our Saviour embodies and enforces the same truth, 'Blessed are the pure in heart: for they shall see God' (*Matt.* 5:8). Let us not, beloved, mistake this character. It is of infinite importance to us that we properly understand it. It is emphatically 'the pure in *heart*', not the informed in judgment, not the reformed in life, not the orthodox in creed, not the apostolic in worship; all these things may exist, as did the outward ritualism of the Pharisees, apart from inward sanctification. But the 'pure in heart' – that is, those whose hearts are sprinkled with the cleansing blood of Jesus, sanctified by the indwelling of the Spirit, growing in a hatred to, and in a disenthralment from, the power of indwelling sin, who feel its existence, mourn its power, loathe its taint, and pray and strive for holiness – such shall see God. They shall see him now in Christ, in the gospel, and in the gracious manifestations of his love. And they shall see him hereafter without a cloud to shade, or a sin to mar, or a sorrow to sadden, or a moment to interrupt the blessed vision.

Oh, with a prospect so full of glory, so near and so certain, who that loves the Saviour would not strive after more of that purity of heart, clad in which and through whose medium we shall behold God forever, as revealed and seen in Christ Jesus? To this end let us welcome God's purifying agent, sanctified trial. When he causes us to walk in the midst of trouble, let us be submissive, humble, and obedient. Resignation to the divine will secures the end God intends to accomplish – our personal and deeper holiness. So long as we cherish an unsubmissive, rebellious spirit, the medicine will not cure, the lesson will not instruct, the agent will not work its mission; in a word, our purity of heart will not be promoted. In the words of Samuel Rutherford, 'When God strikes, let us beware of striking back again; for God will always have the last blow.' When his uplifted hand lights upon us, let us not fly up into his face as the chaff, but fall down at his feet as the wheat. Thus, 'Humble yourselves therefore under the mighty hand of God, that he may exalt you in due time' (1 Pet. 5:6); and in the school of his most trying dispensations we shall learn the sweetest lessons of his love.

Such, then, may be denominated 'the pure in heart'. Perfect freedom from sin, the entire extermination of indwelling evil, root and branch, is not the idea which our Lord here inculcates. This can only be affirmed of Christ himself, of unfallen angels, and of the spirits of just men made perfect. Therefore, let no dear child of God desiring internal holiness, thirsting and struggling for purity of heart, be cast down or discouraged in the conflict by the daily, the hourly consciousness and working of existing impurity. There may be real holiness in the midst of innate unholiness; purity encircled by indwelling impurity; an intense thirst, an ardent prayerfulness for sanctification, and some measure of its attainment, in a soul far, very far, from having arrived at a state of perfect and entire sinlessness. Does not the earnest desire for holiness and the constant struggle for sanctification prove the existence and indwelling power of evil in the saints of God? Most assuredly. And the Lord the Spirit discovers to us more and more of the inbeing and evil of sin, unveils to us more vividly the chambers of abomination, that we may be the more intently set upon the great work of sanctification, that we may deal more closely with Christ's blood and be more earnest and importunate in our cry, 'Create in me a clean heart, O God; and renew a right spirit within me' (*Psa.* 51:10). An old divine wrote,

> As a thing is said to be pure though it may have some dross cleaving to it, as is pure gold when it is digged out of the mine, though there be much dross in it; and we say it is pure air though for a time there be fogs and mists within it; and it is pure water though there be some mud at the bottom; a man may be said to have a pure heart though there be a cleaving of much dross to it. Holy men have a fountain of original corruption in them, and from this fountain sins arise continuously, as the scum in the pot; but as in wine, or honey, or water, though the scum arise, yet still it purifieth itself; contrarily in men of impure hearts the scum ariseth, but it seethes not. 'She hath wearied herself with lies, and her great scum went not forth out of her' (*Ezek.*

24:12). Holy men have their scum arising in their hearts, as well as the wicked; but here is the difference, wicked men's scum seethes in and mingles together, but men of pure heart have a cleansing and purifying disposition, that casts out whatever evil comes, though it be constantly rising. Though it be many times mixed, he still washeth himself again; he cannot endure it; he doth not, as the sinner, delight in it. But notwithstanding this boiling out of evil, he is a man of a pure heart; yet may sin cleave to a man as dross to the silver, but it mingles not with the regenerate heart, nor that mingles with it, no more than oil and water do, which though they touch they do not mingle together.

There is much truth and deep acquaintance with the human heart and the mystery of the divine life in these quaint remarks which may instruct and comfort those of the 'pure in heart' who are often cast down by the working of indwelling sin.

If, then, trial is the believer's pathway to heaven, if the afflictive dealings of our heavenly Father are designed to accelerate our progress in that path, if, in the words of Robert Leighton, 'God never had one son without suffering, and but one without sin,' if in sorrow the Saviour becomes more dear and sin more bitter, and the world is loosened, and the soul, chastened and purified, is matured for glory, if, in a word, this gloomy portal of tribulation through which I pass terminates my night of weeping and ushers me into a world where I shall bask in the young beams of a morning of joy, reap the golden fruit of the seed which often in tears I now sow to the Spirit, lay my weary, panting soul on the bosom of my Saviour, and weep and sigh and sin no more forever, then welcome, thrice welcome, sorrow! Welcome my Saviour's yoke, his burden, his cross! Welcome the discipline of the

covenant, the seal of my sonship, the dealings of my
God! If this be the path to glory, this the evidence of adoption, this the example my Saviour has left me, and this the
help heavenward which sanctified trial brings – the steps
by which I climb, the wings with which I mount, the door
through which I enter as a sinner pardoned through the
blood and justified by the righteousness of Christ – then,
oh then, my Father, thy will, not mine, be done!

Jesus, 'tis my aim divine,
  Hence to have no will but thine;
Let me covenant with thee,
  Thine for evermore to be:
This my prayer, and this alone,
  Saviour, let thy will be done!

Thee to love, to live to thee,
  This my daily portion be;
Nothing to my Lord I give,
  But from him I first receive:
Lord, for me thy blood was spilt,
  Lead me, guide me, as thou wilt.

All that is opposed to thee,
  Howsoever dear it be,
From my heart the idol tear,
  Thou shalt have no rival there;
Only thou shalt fill the throne:
  Saviour, let thy will be done.

Wilt thou, Lord, in me fulfil
  All the pleasure of thy will;
Thine in life, and thine in death,
  Thine in every fleeting breath,
Thou my hope and joy alone:
  Saviour, let thy will be done.

CHAPTER 6

Bonds Loosed

*O LORD, truly I am thy servant; I am thy
servant, and the son of thine handmaid: thou
hast loosed my bonds.*

— Psalm 116:16

In nothing are there found to exist greater opposites,
stronger points of contrast, than in the Christian character. The reason is obvious to a spiritual mind. The
believer is composed of two natures essentially different,
incessantly antagonistic, and eternally irreconcilable.
Nothing can be more diametrically opposed in their
character and actings than the divine and the human,
the renewed and the unrenewed nature that is in the believer. A partaker of the new and divine nature through
grace, and thus a child of God and an heir of heaven, he
still is imprisoned and fettered by the old and fallen nature from which there is no release until the Master
comes and calls for him. Now these two and opposite
natures must be in perpetual hostility the one to the
other. 'What will ye see in the Shulamite? As it were the
company of two armies' (*Song of Sol.* 6:13). Such is the
spectacle which every child of God presents. The existence of these opposite principles of nature and grace, of

sin and holiness, in the same individual must necessarily lead to much that is inexplicable and perplexing to those not thoroughly initiated into the mysteries of the divine life. To the eye of such a one, and not less visible to him within whose heart the conflict rages, there are often apparent discrepancies, contradictions, and opposites in the Christian life of a most painful and embarrassing nature, and thus often bringing those who are weak in faith and but imperfectly instructed in God's Word and the knowledge of themselves into much bondage and distress. They find it difficult, almost impossible, to reconcile these opposites of sin and holiness, these contradictions of grace and nature, with the existence and reality of that higher, nobler, purer nature of which all are partakers who are born of the Spirit, and are new creatures in Christ Jesus. Take as a single illustration of this the subject of the present chapter of our work – the bondage and the liberty, the bonds and the loosening of those bonds, which David delineates as his experience and in which he but portrays the experience, more or less extended, of all the children of God. Here are the two opposites in bold relief exhibited in every believer in the Lord Jesus – bondage and liberty. In proffering you as a Christian pilgrim a little help heavenward, we would be withholding one of the most potent aids in your pilgrim course if we did not endeavour, by the power of the Holy Spirit, to loosen and remove some of those fetters by which so many of the Lord's people are bound, the galling and the weight of which so essentially impede them in their course heavenward.

The ungodly world is full of bondage. The world has its notions of liberty; but we who have tasted the sweetness of Christ's liberty know that its notions are false and that the liberty of which it boasts is only slavery. Every unconverted man and woman is a servant, a slave, a captive. 'Whosoever committeth sin is the servant of sin' (John 8:34). And those who are the servants of sin are, by virtue of that relation, equally the vassals of Satan, 'are taken captive by him at his will' (2 Tim. 2:26). The popular cry is, 'Liberty!' – Liberty of law, liberty of representation, liberty of prescriptive rights, literary and commercial liberty. But do those who vociferate this cry, who demand, and justly too it may be, this freedom know that they are the most degraded of all vassals, that they wear the most galling of all fetters, that they are the willing servants, the obedient slaves, the degraded serfs of the world's fierce despot, Satan? Ah no! 'While they promise them liberty, they themselves are servants of corruption: for of whom a man is overcome, of the same is he brought into bondage' (2 Pet. 2:19). Reader, spiritually you are either a slave or a freeman. You are a slave to an unregenerate nature, a slave of the world, a slave of Satan, a slave of self, a servant of sin, or one whose fetters Christ has wrenched, whose soul Christ has set free.

But the child of God, though a freeman and a partaker of the liberty wherewith Christ makes his people free, may have but a contracted and imperfect view of this liberty, may still walk in much bondage of spirit, re-forge for himself fetters which Christ has broken, and return to those beggarly elements from which Christ has set him free. David was a mighty man of God. Who has read the spiritual exercises of his soul, as delineated in Psalm 119, without the conviction that he was a giant in grace? And yet we find him speaking of bonds. What does this mean? Just simply that a true freeman of the Lord may yet walk in strait paths, may cherish a bound spirit, may be controlled by slavish fear, and may love and serve God with an unfilial, servile mind. Nor can we imagine greater impediments to religious progress, more powerful obstructions in our heavenward course, than just this spiritual bondage which marks the experience of so many. How few look fully into God's face as their Father? How few pray in the spirit of adoption? How few rejoice in the sense of pardoned sin and possess the peace which flows from the justified state procured by the blood and righteousness of our Emmanuel? What numbers are enthralled by their creed, by their church, by their ritual, by their sacraments, by their religious duties, by their crude conceptions of the gospel, their dim views of divine truth, by their faint, defective realization of a personal and complete salvation through Christ? How can such travel with a fleet footstep the heavenly road or mount with a strong and soaring wing the upper skies, chained to earth by bonds like these? Beloved, ye are Christ's freemen; and 'If the Son therefore shall make you free, ye shall be free indeed' (John 8:36). It is to expound more clearly to you what your freedom is, to show more fully your liberty in Christ Jesus, and thus to speed your way heavenward with more of heavenly joy and peace and hope in your soul, that we invite you to consider this fragment of the psalmist's experience, which experience we desire may be yours: 'Thou hast loosed my bonds' (Psa. 116:16).

What a loosening of our bonds is real conversion! Multitudes are yet in the bonds of an unregenerate state who assume that they are converted. There may be a false spiritual as a false natural birth. Many may pass through some of the earlier and incipient stages of conversion – such as the possession of light, and conviction, and alarm, and resolve – and yet not be truly converted. There may be that which has the appearance of the new birth, without the reality. Our Lord most solemnly affirms this of one of the ancient churches, 'Thou hast a name that thou livest, and art dead' (*Rev.* 3:1). Oh, solemn thought! Oh, awful deception! The name of a living soul, the name of a Christian, the name of a disciple of Christ, and yet dead in trespasses and in sins, still in the gall of bitterness and the bond of iniquity, with not a loosed fetter that bound the soul to self-righteousness, to the love of the world, and to the captivity of Satan and of sin. But in true conversion the bonds are loosed. Christ touches them, and they are broken. One gentle pressure of his divine hand, and the soul is free. 'For the law of the Spirit of life in Christ Jesus hath made me free from the law of sin and death' (*Rom.* 8:2). Oh, what a blessed freedom from the burden of guilt is this which Jesus gives! The moment Christ is seen to be the 'end of the law for righteousness to every one that believeth' (*Rom.* 10:4) – the moment the burden of sin is laid upon him, the atoning blood touches the conscience, the Holy Spirit testifies of Jesus as bearing all the sin, enduring all the punishment, and exhausting all the curse – the believing soul bursts its fetters and enters into that liberty with which Christ makes his people free.

Beloved, cannot you say, in view of this truth: Christ hath loosed my bonds? I once wore the chain of my sins, and the galling yoke of the law, and the heavy manacles of a poor captive of Satan; but Jesus saw me and had compassion, and said, 'Loose him, and let him go' (*John* 11:44); and my grave-clothes fell off, my bonds were broken, and I sprang into the holy liberty of a sinner pardoned, justified, and forever saved; and my soul overflowed with 'joy unspeakable and full of glory' (1 *Pet.* 1:8). The bliss of that moment, the sweetness of that first taste of liberty, can I ever forget! Truly the sacred poet depicts my feelings:

> *That sweet comfort was mine,*
> > *When the favour divine*
> *I received through the blood of the Lamb;*
> > *When my heart first believed,*
> *What a joy I received,*
> > *What a heaven in Jesus' name!*

> *'Twas a heaven below*
> > *My Redeemer to know;*
> *And the angels could do nothing more*
> > *Than to fall at his feet,*
> *And the story repeat,*
> > *And the Lover of sinners adore.*

> *Jesus all the day long*
> > *Was my joy and my song:*
> *Oh that all his salvation might see!*
> > *He hath loved me, I cried,*
> *He hath suffer'd and died,*
> > *To redeem even rebels like me.*

> *On the wings of his love,*
> > *I was carried above*
> *All sin, and temptation, and pain;*
> > *And I could not believe*
> *That I ever should grieve,*
> > *That I ever should suffer again.*

When the Spirit's seal of adoption is impressed upon the heart, there is a loosening of the bonds of legality in which so many of God's children are held. How jealous is the Holy Ghost of the glory and enjoyment of our sonship! Listen to his language: 'As many as are led by the

Spirit of God, they are the sons of God. For ye have not received the spirit of bondage again to fear; but ye have received the Spirit of adoption, whereby we cry, Abba, Father. The Spirit itself beareth witness with our spirit, that we are the children of God' (*Rom.* 8:14–16). Do you ask, my reader, what is a legal spirit from which the Spirit of adoption frees us? I answer, it is that bondage which springs from looking within yourself for evidences, for comfort, and for motives which only can be found in looking to Jesus. It is that spirit of legality which prompts you to be incessantly poring over your works, instead of dealing simply and solely with the finished work of Christ. That is a spirit of bondage which makes a Christ of duties and labours and sacrifices, of tears and confessions and faith, rather than directly and supremely dealing with him 'who of God is made unto us wisdom, and righteousness, and sanctification, and redemption' (*1 Cor.* 1:30).

Beloved, your works, your doing, your sacrifices, as means of comfort and as grounds of hope, are nothing but filthy rags, the bones of the skeleton, the chaff which the wind scatters. Why have you not joy and peace and hope in believing? Simply because, unsuspected by yourself, you are putting your own work in the place of Christ's work. Oh that you may be led to cast yourself more entirely upon the atoning sacrifice of Jesus; to believe that God looks not at a single work you do as justifying you in his sight, but that he looks only to the divine, sacrificial, flawless, perfect work of his beloved Son! Oh, come and rest where God rests, in the Crucified One! If he is pleased to accept you in his Son, are you not satisfied so to be accepted? If the blood and righteousness of Emmanuel are enough for God, are they not enough also for you? Away, then, with your fears and distrust and bondage, and enter fully into Christ! 'Even so would he have removed thee out of the strait into a broad place, where there is no straitness; and that which should be set on thy table should be full of fatness' (*Job* 36:16). Then shall you exclaim, 'Thou hast loosed my bonds.'

A sealed sense of pardoned sin gives liberty to the soul. Many of the Lord's people walk in bonds from not seeing how fully and freely and entirely their sins are pardoned. If Christ has borne and has pardoned all your sins, then you have nothing to do with them. If he was condemned, suffered, died, and rose again for our offences, if he bore them, satisfied for them, and by one blood-shedding forever blotted them out, what have you, who believe in him, to do with those sins which he has eternally obliterated, 'having forgiven you all trespasses' (*Col.* 2:13)? Will you attempt to remove the propitiation, the mercy-seat, which covers them? Will you endeavor to recall the thick cloud which his blood has forever cancelled? Will you look into the tomb, or sink your line into the sea, where Jesus has left all your transgressions? Oh, this will be to seek another sacrifice for sin, to crucify the Son of God afresh, to deny the efficacy of his blood, and to cast a veil over the brightest lustre of his cross. Thy sins *are* forgiven thee! Thou hast no more to do with them than with a criminal who has been arraigned, condemned, and executed. Jesus stood as our Sin-bearer, Surety, and Substitute; he was arraigned, and condemned, and crucified in our stead, and for our sin. 'He was wounded for our transgressions, he was bruised for our iniquities' (*Isa.* 53:5).

We have, therefore, nothing to do with the con-

demning power of our sins, for God's own Son was
made 'in the likeness of sinful flesh, and for sin' (or by a
sacrifice for sin) 'condemned sin in the flesh' (*Rom.* 8:3);
so that, if condemnation and guilt be removed, it is our
privilege to walk in the holy, happy blessedness of the
man whose transgression is forgiven, whose sin is covered, unto whom the Lord imputeth not iniquity. Let
your life be a daily exercise of faith in the atoning, sin-
pardoning blood of Jesus touching the guilt and power
of sin, and with David, you shall gratefully exclaim,
'Thou hast loosed my bonds'.

The Lord also looses the bonds of those of his people
who are 'bound in fetters, and be holden in cords of affliction' (*Job* 36:8). How many are wearing these fetters!
The Lord trieth the righteous, but he does not leave
them in their trials. And again, 'Many are the afflictions
of the righteous: but the LORD delivereth him out of
them all' (*Psa.* 34:19). Listen, too, to the testimony of
David, 'I called upon the LORD in distress: the LORD answered me, and set me in a large place' (*Psa.* 118:5). He
broke the bonds of my affliction and brought me into liberty. When we take a legal and not a gospel view of
affliction, view it as the punishment of the slave and not
as the chastening of the child, as judicial and not parental, we are brought into bondage. Oh, is it not enough
that we are bound in fetters and are holden in cords of
affliction, that we should add to these bonds those of
unfilial submission, secret rebellion, restiveness, and repining? Oh, how we lose the soothing and the comfort,
the succour, and the liberty in deep and sore trial by not
tracing it all up to a Father's hand, a Saviour's love, the
arrangement and provision of the covenant of grace.

Tried believer, were you now to lean with all your

burdens on the Lord, to rest on Jesus, to wait patiently in all your perplexities and difficulties for God, oh, in what a large place would you walk! Could you in the over-shadowing cloud, in this heavy calamity, in this sudden visitation, but realize that all God's thoughts are peace, and that every thought of his heart is love, and that all his dealings are right, that as a father pitieth his children, so he pitieth you, oh, how light would be these fetters, how silken these cords, how fragrant the blossoms upon this rod! 'O God of my righteousness: thou hast enlarged me when I was in distress' (*Psa.* 4:1). Enlarged me when in distress! Yes, beloved; God, your own God, can en-large your heart and free your spirit even in distress! What enlargement in prayer, what travelling up of your soul to him in communion, what soaring of your heart in love, what mounting upon the wing of faith, may you now experience and enjoy, though through fire and through water God may be bringing you! I believe that our heavenly Father often binds us with the fetters of trial and the cords of affliction that our soul might be more fully brought into the liberty of adoption. It is in the nar-row path of difficulty and sorrow that we often walk in the broad path of God's love. It is only in the school of sorrow that we learn the holiest and highest of all lessons, the lesson of resignation to the divine will. It is when the cup touches our lips, that from them breathe the sacred words, 'Not my will, but thine, be done' (*Luke* 22:42).

> *Let me never choose – to live or die;*
> *Bind or bruise, in thy hands I lie.*

The Lord loosens our bonds when we walk in evan-gelical obedience. Nothing contributes more to the enlargement of the soul in the ways of the Lord than a profound and practical reverence for the authority and teaching of Christ. Christ is the great political or governing Head and King of his church; and all who recognize the rule, headship, and sovereignty of the Lord Jesus in Zion are solemnly bound to yield obedience to his laws. In so doing, he makes them to walk in a large place. 'If ye be willing and obedient, ye shall eat the good of the land' (*Isa.* 1:19). Obedience to Christ and the liberty of Christ are correlative terms. It is in submitting to his yoke and in bearing his burden that true freedom is found. Many are wearily dragging along their pilgrimage the bonds of doubt and fear simply because of willful disobedience to the divine precepts and positive commands of their Lord and Master. They walk not in the liberty of the child because they walk not in the precept of the disciple. But what was David's experience? 'I will walk at liberty: for I seek thy precepts' (*Psa.* 119:45).

This preceptive obedience, many, wise in their own conceit, denounce as legalism and bondage; but the psalmist felt it to be the sweetest and holiest liberty. The Lord keep you from antinomianism in every form, in doctrine and in practice! Listen again to the words of David in which he strikingly incorporates his servitude and freedom: 'O LORD, truly I am thy servant...thou hast loosed my bonds.' To be the Lord's servant, is to be the Lord's freeman, for Christ's service is perfect freedom. It is a service growing out of freedom, and it is a freedom found in service. O Lord, I am thy servant! Thou hast freed me from the bonds of sin and Satan, and now my highest honour, and my dearest delight, and my most perfect freedom is in serving thee! Is not every heart which is touched by the emancipating, all-constraining power of Christ's love responsive to this? 'That he would grant unto us, that we being delivered out of the hand of our enemies might serve him without fear, in holiness and righteousness before him, all the days of our life' (*Luke* 1:74–75). Would you then, Christian pilgrim, speed your way heavenward? Burst the bonds which so long have hindered your loving obedience to Christ, the fear of man, the opinion of the world, the love of earthly repose – come, take up your cross, and follow him. Lord, dost thou ask obedience to thy precepts as the proof of my love to thee? Then I will follow thee whithersoever thou goest. Dissolve thou my fetters, loosen my bonds, for then 'I will run the way of thy commandments, when thou shalt enlarge my heart' (*Psa.* 119:32).

'O Lord, I am the son of thine handmaid.' Sacred and precious acknowledgment! Advanced to the kingdom of Israel though he was, David did not yet forget his relation and indebtedness to a God-fearing mother. The early instruction and prayers of that mother were the basis of all his future greatness, and were now treasured among his most precious recollections. With the incense of gratitude ascending from his heart for the loosing of his bonds, he blesses the hallowed remembrance of a godly parent and offers devout thanksgiving to God for that sacred and precious gift. How clearly the future holy and honourable freedom from the appetites of the flesh, and from the slavishness of the world, and from the captivity of opinions, skeptical and loose, which distinguishes the high and noble career of many a man renowned in the Church of Christ and in the world, may be traced to the early, hidden links of a Christian mother's training and prayers, eternity only can declare. Nor let us forget that when our hearts are charged with grief, and our path is lonely, and our need is pressing, the hallowed recollection of all that God was in his faithfulness, and kindness, and responsive love to the voice of prayer breathing from a godly parent's lips, may encourage us to pray and may furnish us with a more urgent plea at the throne of grace, the tenderness and force of which even God will not resist. 'O LORD, truly I am thy servant; I am thy servant, and the son of thine handmaid: thou hast loosed my bonds.' Such is the undying influence of a godly parent – a Christian, praying mother!

Are you, beloved, all your lifetime in bondage through the fear of death? Alas, how this impedes your happy, joyful progress heavenward! But Jesus can loosen, and virtually has loosened, these bonds. He reminds you that you are to contemplate not death, but his personal and glorious coming. If your thoughts will wander from this bright and blessed hope to the more gloomy and repulsive object of your departure to him, you are to remember that he has vanquished death and has passed through the grave as your Substitute, your Surety, your Head; that he has extracted the venom of the one and has irradiated the gloom of the other; and that you have no sting to apprehend and no shadows to dread, because he has passed that way before you.

Moreover, he has pledged his most loving and most faithful word that when you tread the valley, solitary and alone as you must be, you shall fear no evil, for that he, your risen, living Lord and Saviour, will be with you. Lo, I am with you always! Then, why hug these chains, why wear these bonds, when simple, unquestioning faith in this your Lord's assurance – and, oh, he is worthy of your love's implicit confidence! – would disenthral you? Perhaps with you life is ebbing, earth's toils and scenes are fading, and the ties that bind you here are breaking one by one, but that one fetter still enslaves you, the most painful and the heaviest of all, the fear of death! Oh, turn your eye to Jesus, with whom your soul is in living and inseparable union; Jesus, your life-creating, life-keeping Head; one glance, one touch, and your fears are dissolved and your fettered spirit is free! What, will Christ be enough for life, its trial, its sorrows, its changes, its sins, and not be equal, in the supports of his grace, in the comfort of his love, and in the sunshine of his presence, for the sinkings, the becloudings, the partings, the throb and throe of death? Away with such suspicion and distrust! How dishonouring to him who so loved you as to part with the last drop of blood and the last pulse of life! Sick, sinking, dying believer, your Saviour is near! The present moment may find the cold chill of adversity stealing over you, perchance forsaken and neglected, lone and sad. But why these fears? Jesus is near, oh, how near, nearer than ever at this moment! His sheltering wing flutters over you; the warm pavilion of his heart encircles you. Compose the ruffled pinions of your redeemed soul for its glorious flight. Take a firm, clinging, unyielding hold of the Strong One, the Ransoming One, the Faithful One, the Near and Precious One, and you need fear no evil. Oh, what a hiding-place is Christ!

> *'Tis chilly; very chilly;*
> *And 'tis dark!*
> *There is no light in friendship's eye;*
> *On the heart's hearth*
> *No spark.*
>
> *Let me draw near — my Saviour,*
> *Oh, so near!*
> *Let me once feel thy tender smile —*

Thine own sweet smile
Of cheer.

Let one fold of thy garment
   Wrap me round:
Ah! blessed, happy spirit, now
   Thy joy, thy bliss,
   Is found!

Let us beware of self-imposed bonds. Christ binds us with no fetters but love and imposes no bonds but that submission which is our most perfect freedom. His gracious mission to our world was to break every bond and to let the oppressed go free. The Spirit of the Lord God was upon him, because the Lord anointed him to proclaim liberty to the captive and the opening of the prison to them that are bound. By his power the prey is snatched from the mighty, the lawful captive is delivered, and a door in heaven is opened to the prisoners of hope. He himself became a bond-servant that we might become children and a captive that we might be free. Oh, was ever love so vast, so self-sacrificing as this? We repeat the caution: forge for your soul no bonds but those which God imposes, which grace binds, and which love, obedient and willing, cheerfully wears for Christ. You are free to pray, free to enter with holy boldness and filial openness into the most holy place; you are free to claim and appropriate all the blessings of the covenant, and to draw boundlessly from the fulness of the Saviour. You are free to bring every sin to his atonement, and every sorrow to his sympathy, and every burden to his shoulder. You are free to follow the footsteps of the flock, to feed where they are pastured, and to lie down where they repose. You are free to go in and out of the one

Church of your Father, and to find a home, a temple, and a banquet-house wherever you realize the presence of the Master or recognize the features of the disciple. The one church of which you are a member is the 'Jerusalem which is above [which] is free, which is the mother of us all' (*Gal.* 4:26). Beloved, you are called unto liberty; use it fully, use it holily.

You complain of bondage in prayer. Never, perhaps, are you so sensible of the chafing of the fetters as when you retire from the presence of man into the solemn presence of God. Oh, could you but then be free! Could you but pour out an unfettered heart, moved, prompted, and enlarged by God's free Spirit, how happy would you be! But no. You cannot pray. You have no wants, no desires, no emotions: thoughts seem stifled in their birth, words freeze upon your lips, and you rise from your knees as one whose devotions have been but as the chattering of the swallow.

But why are you thus fettered? Are not these bonds your own creating? Are you not endeavouring to excite and rouse your own feelings, rather than seeking the influence of the Holy Spirit? Are you not relying upon your own intellectual efforts, instead of seeking to offer to God the sacrifice of a broken heart and a contrite spirit? Are you not bending your eye within and upon yourself, rather than looking from off and out of self, simply and only to Jesus? Do you not come with the self-sufficient spirit of the Pharisee, rather than in the self-condemning spirit of the publican? Do you not approach God as a claimer of his regard, rather than as the petitioner of his bounty; as rich and full and indifferent, rather than as poor and needy and earnest? But listen to God's remedy, 'Be filled with the Spirit' (*Eph.* 5:18). He is especially promised to burst your bonds in prayer (*Rom.* 8:26). Breathing upon them his all-divine, all-potent influence, all, one by one, will dissolve, and you shall 'come boldly unto the throne of grace, that [you] may obtain mercy, and find grace to help in time of need' (*Heb.* 4:16). Again do I earnestly exhort you to cast yourself in prayer upon the love and power of the Holy Ghost, beseeching him to give you to feel your soul's emptiness and poverty, and then, with that truth sealed upon your heart, to lead you to the fulness and sufficiency of Christ. One gracious touch of the Spirit, one application of the atoning blood, one dim sight of the cross, one gentle word of the Saviour, and your bonds are broken, and your soul is free. 'Where the Spirit of the Lord is, there is liberty' (2 *Cor.* 3:17). Let this be your prayer, importunately urged, until fully answered: 'Bring my soul out of prison, that I may praise thy name.' And for your encouragement in prayer, I would remind you of the promise, 'The LORD heareth the poor, and despiseth not his prisoners' (*Psa.* 69:33).

Dwell much in holy and cheerful anticipation of the glorious and perfect enfranchisement which yet awaits your soul. It speedeth on! Oh, what a deliverance to you will be the coming of the Lord, should not the Lord anticipate it by death, the covenant-messenger! Then will you, oh prisoners of hope, be emancipated from indwelling sin, from all mental beclouding and bodily infirmity, and in the twinkling of an eye, your spirit will breathe the sweet air of liberty, and in a world of wonder, glory, and love, with unfettered and untiring wing, expatiate in the range and sweep of its ever-widening, ever-receding horizon. That spirit, now free, will, at the trump of the archangel, descend and reunite itself with the slumbering dust, the dust that sleeps in Jesus, which shall then be reanimated and 'delivered from the bondage of corruption' (*Rom.* 8:21), 'fashioned like unto his glorious body' (*Phil.* 3:21); and then, and forever, the last link will be broken that bound me, O sin and death, to thee!

Holy Lord God! I love thy truth,
   Nor dare thy least commandment slight,
Yet, pierced by sin, the serpent's tooth,
   I mourn the anguish of the bite.

But though the poison lurks within,
   Hope bids me still with patience wait,
Till death shall set me free from sin,
   Free from the only thing I hate.

Had I a throne above the rest,
   Where angels and archangels dwell,
One sin, unslain, within my breast,
   Would make that heaven as dark as hell.

The prisoner sent to breathe fresh air,
   And bless'd with liberty again,
Would mourn were he condemn'd to wear
   One link of all his former chain.

But oh, no foe invades the bliss,
   Where glory crowns the Christian's head;
One view of Jesus as he is,
   Will strike all sin forever dead.

CHAPTER 7

Human Care
Transferred to God

Casting all your care upon him; for he careth for you.
—1 Peter 5:7

Were we to take the world's estimate of the real value and happiness of a life of faith in God as the true one, how gloomy, joyless, and forlorn a life would it appear! The world imagines that there is nothing substantial, bright, or social in the religion of Christ – no reality, sunshine, or companionship. But how mistaken! We cite as disproving this view the precept we propose in this chapter which enjoins the transfer of human care to God. Where in the world's wilderness, grows the flower of heart's ease as it blooms and blossoms here? 'Casting all your care upon him; for he careth for you.' How full of soothing and repose are these words! What cares have they lightened, what anxieties have they removed, what burdens have they unclasped, what springs of joy and comfort and hope have they unsealed in many a sad and oppressed heart!

But do you not, beloved reader, need to be put in constant remembrance of this divine secret of rest amidst toil, of repose amidst disquietude, of soothing amidst corroding cares, and of confidence and hope in the midst of change and depression? Bewildered and oppressed by the multitude of anxious thoughts within you, is there not a danger of being so absorbed by the care as to overlook the Care-taker, to forget the heart's ease in the overwhelming of the heart's anxiety? Verily we think so. Hagar, pining with thirst and blinded by grief, saw not the well of water flowing at her side. The disciples in the storm, filled with alarm and absorbed by fear, recognized not the Lord Jesus walking to them upon the waves which threatened the foundering of their vessel.

Thus often is it with us; thus may it be now with you. We look at the want, and not at him who supplies it; at the storm, and not at him who controls it; at the care, and not at him who assumes it. Is not the voice of the Lord mightier than the voice of many waters, yea, than the mighty waves of the sea? Is not the Care-taker greater than the care itself? Yet how we limit the Holy One and magnify and multiply our cares, anxieties, and sorrows! But for the immutability of our redeeming God, whose unseen hand guides and whose power, almost insensible to ourselves, sustains us, our care would consume us. How often we are upheld, we scarcely know how; preserved in safety, we scarcely know why. But 'the secret of the LORD is with them that fear him' (*Psa.* 25:14); and sooner or later, we learn that Jesus has done it all, and has done it for his own glory. I desire, beloved reader, to proffer you a little help heavenward by inciting you to this transfer of anxious thought and chafing care to God. Lightened a little of your burden, with a more trustful heart and gladsome spirit, you will speed your way homeward to that heaven of perfect repose, upon whose threshold you will leave the last anxious thought and lay down the last earthly care, your weary, panting soul pillowed in eternal repose.

The world through which we pass heavenward – and oh, forget not, Christian pilgrim, it is a passage soon passed – is a world laden and crushed with care. Earthly care confronts at every step and in all whom we meet. The knitted brow, the restless eye, the compressed lip, the fevered expression, the bated breath, are as true an index of the mind oppressed with anxious thought, the heart shaded with human sorrow, as the dial is of the sun's altitude. It is true the great device of the world is to conceal its care from others. But its transient gleam of artificial joy – the forced smile, the excited laugh, the unnatural levity, which imparts an air of happiness and freedom from eating care – betrays to the keen, penetrating eye of the spiritual observer that inward restlessness of the spirit, that lowering anxiety of mind, which can ill be concealed.

> *If every man's internal care*
> *Were written on his brow,*
> *How many would our pity share*
> *Who move our envy now!*

But it is of the care peculiar to the Lord's own people that we particularly speak. And here we must be cautious to distinguish between the carefulness that is proper in a child of God and the carefulness which is the result of a distrust of God, the offspring of unbelief. We are to be careful, undoubtedly, to maintain good works, or our faith is vain; to take care of our own house, or we shall be found worse than the infidel; we are to care for the interests and prosperity of Christ's church, or we ignore our individual membership; we are to be careful to walk holily and circumspectly, as followers of the Lamb, or we dishonour Christ. Now this implies a heavy weight of holy care, unslumbering vigilance, and unceasing prayerfulness on our part. These are cares which especially appertain to, and are inseparable from, our Christianity. But let us consider that state of anxious carefulness which so much weighs down the spirit, so beclouds our spiritual joy, and is so corrosive of the best, holiest, and finest feelings of the soul, but which a simple childlike confidence in our heavenly Father's promise, care, and love should chasten and moderate, yea, entirely remove. Hence the precept, 'Casting all your care upon him; for he careth for you'.

We may attempt to classify, but it would be impossible to enumerate, the cares which contribute so much to the mental anxiety and depression of the Christian. The cares of this life enter deeply into the carefulness of which the Lord seeks to lighten us. In proportion to the spiritual tone of the mind and the closeness of the heart's converse with God and heavenly realities will be the tenderness of the believer to the chafing and pressure of temporal cares. The more heavenly we grow, the more acutely sensitive do we become to the encroachment and influence of earth and earthly things.

In this connection let me remark that I fear too little prayerful consideration is felt by the church in behalf of her Christian men of business. Sustaining responsibilities, burdened with cares, depressed by anxieties well-nigh crushing – earnestly desirous, and that very desire intensifying their feelings, that integrity and uprightness should preserve them, that by no faltering, no receding, no departure from the strictest line of Christian consistency should the cause of Christ be dishonoured and their Christian character be compromised – are they sufficiently borne upon our sympathies and prayers? Do we, in measure, make their burden, their dangers, their anxieties our own? Do we ask for them of God the grace that will keep them in prosperity and for the strength and comfort that will sustain and soothe them under the pressure and perils of anxious care? Does the Church of God sufficiently sympathize with her Christian merchants? May not the low standard of commercial morality, which in some departments of trade has obtained in this and other lands, the sad defection from honesty, probity, and uprightness which has marked the business transactions of some whose names have stood high in the church's roll, the frauds, the misappropriations, the nefarious dealings, be traceable, in a great degree, to the church's unfaithfulness in her duty respecting them? Verily we think so.

Oh, let us pray more for godly men of business! Their snares are many, their perils are great, their cares are crushing, their anxieties are absorbing! They demand our Christian sympathy, our tender forbearance, our unceasing supplications, that in all the temptations and intricacies, perils and anxieties by which their path is beset, God may hold them up and conduct them through, kept from the low arts of trade, from the questionable practices of the world, from an inordinate anxiety for wealth, from even the slightest deviation from the straightest and strictest line of Christian integrity, from the taint and evil of the world, to the honour of the church and the glory of their Lord. Christian brethren, we proffer you our sympathy and breathe on your behalf our prayers! You may often lay an anxious, aching brow on your pillow at night, not knowing how you will meet the stern claims of the coming day – your commercial standing, and dearer still, your Christian character, at stake. Be still! There is One who careth for you. Compose yourself to rest, in the calm assurance that on the morrow God will crown your obedience to the precept by his fulfilment of the promise, 'Casting all your care upon him; for he careth for you'.

Thus, then, our temporal cares, to us often so depressing, are objects of God's consideration. If godliness has the promise of the life that now is, it follows that no earthly care that saddens the heart or shades the brow is beneath his notice or regard. How many a child of God is struggling with large domestic claims and but slender revenues! Who can tell the troubled thoughts, the anxious feelings, the painful forebodings that pass through that mind! One only knows it. To him there is nothing little, nothing insignificant, nothing beneath his notice and regard. Are you a widow, with narrowed income and heavy demands? Are you an orphan, combating loneliness and want? Are you a man of business, sustaining heavy liabilities, involved in perilous investments, and weighed down by ceaseless anxiety and care? Veiled from every eye but God's may be your pressure. These worldly engagements, these temporal cares and anxieties, are not too insignificant for him.

Then, there often presses upon the heart the anxiety to know the path of duty in which we should walk. This is no small care to the child of God. We are often brought to a stand still and are, as it were, at our wits' end. Two paths intersecting each other, diverging to the right and to the left, confront us, and we are perplexed to know which one we should take. Oh for a voice, distinct and familiar, behind us, saying, 'This is the way, walk ye in it' (*Isa.* 30:21)! In proportion, too, to the tenderness of conscience and to the closeness and softness of the walk, will be the intense anxiety of the mind to know, and do, and even suffer the will of God. If such be the case with you, be assured that though your faith and patience may be tried, the Lord will not leave you long in darkness and uncertainty. If the question be, 'How shall I know the will of my heavenly Father in this matter?' you shall not in the end mistake it; for God cares for you.

But there are greater cares than these, the spiritual care of the soul, which often press heavily upon the heart. You are anxious to know that you have an interest in Christ's redeeming love, that your name is written among the living in Jerusalem, that your sins are pardoned, that your person is adopted, accepted, saved, and that after death you will reign with Jesus forever. You are anxious, too, that your Christian walk should be obedient, principled, believing; that you should be more heavenly minded, growing in knowledge, and grace, and divine conformity to the will of God and the image of Jesus. Ah, these are cares before which all others vanish into insignificance! There are no anxieties, no cares, no burdens like those which touch the present and future interests and well-being of the soul. How many a man would freely and joyfully part with all his worldly possessions for spiritual peace of mind and for an assured hope of the future! Oh to be quite sure that we are saved! What is rank, what is wealth, what is learning, what is fame in comparison with this, but the dust, the foam, the dream, the shadow!

Anxious soul, do you think that you nurse that spiritual anxiety alone – that no eye is wakeful to see, that no ear is bending to listen, that no heart is interested to sympathize? Ah, yes! He who travailed in sorrow for your salvation is personally, tenderly cognizant of the anxious, the profoundly anxious, desire of your soul that there may not rest the shadow of a shade of doubt and uncertainty upon the fact of its everlasting safety. You are not alone in this soul-exercise. Jesus is with you. The travail of your heart after him, the panting of your spirit for his salvation, the longing of your soul for an assured interest in his love, your tears, your sighs, your desires, your prayers, your watchings, awaken in the heart of your Saviour the deepest, tenderest response. Ah! if the cares, anxieties, and solicitude you feel for your soul lie upon your heart with a pressure so intense as to shade the sunshine of life by day and to bedew your pillow with tears by night, do you think that he does not yet more closely entwine your precious and deathless interests around his heart, who bought you upon the cross, who wearily trod many a step to seek and find you in the cloudy and dark day, and who will deck his brow with you as a sparkling jewel, when he cometh having on his head his many crowns?

But upon whom is the believer to place this care? There is no difficulty in determining. The transfer is at once from the human to the divine, from the finite to the infinite. We have but one true Burden-bearer, one almighty Care-taker, even him whom God has made strong for himself and strong for us, the mighty and the almighty Saviour. In the matter of care the Lord would have us deal immediately and only with himself. This is the controversy he has with us – our unwillingness to make the transfer to him. Oh, could you be assured that

the friend you best loved on earth could lighten the burden and chase away the care, ere the evening's sun had
set, would you not be found breathing your sorrows into
his ear and reposing your anxieties upon his heart? But
to go to God, to pass by the human and deal only with
the divine, to repair to the arm that was transfixed and
to the bosom that bled upon the cross, and repose your
burden upon its power and love, oh, how difficult – just
because it is faith dealing with the invisible! And yet no
task so easy or in its issue, more blessed – just because it
is faith dealing with the Mighty One. But God, watchful
for his honour, will not yield this controversy and, jealous of his love, will not abate an iota of his claim. To him
the transfer must be made.

Behold the key that unlocks the mystery of his dealings! Why has he smitten as with paralysis that arm
upon which you leaned? Why has he chilled as with
death that bosom on which you reclined? Why has he exhausted as by a burning drought that cool spring whose
tide you quaffed? Why has he beclouded those sunny
slopes, upheaved those verdant banks which gave to the
landscape of your life an aspect so picturesque and to
life itself a repose and a charm so exquisite? Oh, but to
win, and woo, and draw you more closely beneath his
own outstretched arm, and within his own sheltering
bosom! He and he alone will share, and by sharing will
soothe and exhaust your care. Christ loves you too well,
has bought you with a price too dear, has entwined you
with interests too costly and precious, and has prepared
for you a heaven and a destiny too glorious and lasting,
to admit a rival or unite with a partner in this office of
Care-taker of the church. Oh, thank him for clearing the
path by removing so kindly and so gently the object that

intercepted your approach to him, so that no angel, no saint, no minister, no church, no friend, should come between Christ and you, veiling him for an instant or in the slightest degree from your eye.

But you will ask, 'How is this transfer of care to be made?' In the directions which we suggest we would give prominence to the exercise of unquestioning faith. Here there must be a taking God at his word. Our warrant for an act apparently so impossible and presumptuous as the transferring of every thought of anxiety, and feeling of sadness, and pressure of want, to the great Jehovah must be as divine and unquestionable as the act itself. That warrant is God's revealed, infallible, unalterable word – 'Cast thy burden upon the LORD, and he shall sustain thee' (*Psa.* 55:22). Your faith must credit, receive, trust in, and act upon this word without demur or condition, immediately and unreservedly, because it is the word of the living God! You must believe that God's power is able, and that his love is willing, and that his grace is sufficient to assume the transfer; that Christ, who has borne the heavier pressure of your curse, and your sins, and your very hell, is prepared to sustain, succour, and comfort you, removing your burden of care by absorbing it in himself.

O wondrous act! O precious life of faith! How happy to us, how glorifying to God! Beloved, can you not, will you not, believe that Jesus at this moment stands prepared to make all your care his own, that he means what he says when he invites you, the weary and the heavy-laden, to himself for rest? Do you think that he is taunting your sorrow, sporting with your care, trifling with your feelings, mocking your confidence, and asking you to believe, only that he might betray; to trust, only to de-

ceive? Oh no! This is not the Christ of the Bible. Did he
ever deal thus with a poor sinner? Was it ever known
that he invited to his feet an anxious, care-depressed,
burdened soul but to spurn that soul from his presence?
Never! Oh, he is too true, too loving, too gentle, too
kind, too faithful a Saviour for that! Will you, then,
wound him with your doubts, dishonour him by your
unbelief, and force from under you, buffeted as you are
amidst the waves, this divine, sustaining plan of faith in
the Word and promise of the only true and living God?

Prayer is no less potent as a means of transferring
care to God. God often sends the care to arouse us to call
upon him. We want an errand, and he sends a trial; we
want an impulse, and he sends a sorrow; we want earnestness and importunity, and he sends the heavy and
the continuous stroke, all his waves breaking over us.
Prayer is the safety-valve of the soul. The heart would
break, the spirit would sink, despair would fold its dark
shroud around us, but for the privilege of access to God
through Christ. Many a burdened believer has exclaimed, 'Why sit I here nursing in lonely grief my
sorrow? I will arise and give myself to prayer'. And the
moment he has formed the resolution, before he has
presented or even framed his petition, unutterable relief
has come. 'When my heart is overwhelmed: lead me to
the rock that is higher than I' (*Psa.* 61:2).

What, then, is your sorrow? Is it sin? Arise, and in
prayer pour out your confession to Christ, and cast this
burden on the Sin-bearer. Is it temptation? Disclose it to
him who was once tempted too, and by the same tempter,
and who thus, from experience of what they feel, knows
how to succour them that are tempted. Is it want? Betake
yourself to the throne of grace and let your requests be

made known unto God, and in quick and ample response he will supply all your need. Oh, try the experiment of prayer! All others may have failed you – try yet this one! Spread your care before the Lord. His providence and grace stand pledged to meet your every necessity.

> *Hast thou a care, whose presence dread*
> *Expels sweet slumbers from thy bed?*
> *To thy Redeemer take that care,*
> *And turn anxiety to prayer.*
>
> *Hast thou a wish, with which thy heart*
> *Would feel it almost death to part?*
> *Entreat thy God that wish to crown,*
> *Or give thee strength to lay it down.*
>
> *Hast thou a friend, whose image dear*
> *May prove an idol worshipp'd here?*
> *Implore thy God that nought may be*
> *A shadow between heaven and thee.*
>
> *Whate'er the wish that breaks thy rest,*
> *Whate'er the care that swells thy breast,*
> *Spread before God that wish, that care,*
> *And turn anxiety to prayer.*

'He careth for you.' Such is the encouragement to a compliance with his holy precept. The care of God extends over all. 'Thou openest thine hand, and satisfiest the desire of every living thing' (*Psa.* 145:16). 'Thou givest them their meat in due season' (*Psa.* 145:15). Oh, what a God is our God! But if such is God's goodness to his enemies, for he maketh his sun to shine on the evil and the good, what must be his goodness to his children? If he has regard to the raven and feeds it when it cries, will he, do you think, be indifferent to the plaintive note of his dove, his undefiled one? It is a special care with which God cares for you. He cares for your temporal interests; not one worldly anxiety, not one want of the life that now is, is too insignificant for his regard. He cares for your spiritual interests, for your soul's prosperity, for your mental peace, for your joy of heart, for your growth in grace, for your character, your reputation, your usefulness. It is personal care. He cares for *you*. He cares for your individual cares, for your personal interests, never for an instant merging and forgetting your individual claims upon his interest, protection, and love in the great body of his church. What encouragement this is to betake yourself to the Lord, transferring all care from your heart to his! Let me conclude this chapter with one or two cautionary observations.

Do not anticipate care. This is to exceed the limit which God has prescribed. With the future you have no concern, as you have no knowledge. A covenant God has from eternity provided for that future. It is all in the everlasting covenant of grace and will unfold and assume just that form and complexion which your God sees best. By anticipating care and thus antedating your future, you grieve the Spirit of God, wound your own peace, and unfit yourself for present duty and trial. When that care comes, if come it should, it will bring with it its own support and a fulfilment of the promise, 'He careth for you'.

Sit not brooding over your state, deploring its existence and lamenting your lack of more faith, and grace, and love. Arise, be responsive to the precept and cast your burden upon the Lord, and he will sustain both you and it. This inordinate absorption with yourself will bring to you no relief, no heart's ease, and no nourishment to faith. One uplifted glance, one sight of Jesus, one believing touch of the promise of God, will bring more repose to your anxious spirit, more succour to your burdened mind, than a lifetime of self-absorption.

>*No profit canst thou gain*
>>*By self-consuming care;*
>*To him commend thy cause, his ear*
>>*Attends the softest prayer.*
>
>*Give to the winds thy fears;*
>>*Hope, and be undismay'd;*
>*God hears thy sighs, and counts thy tears,*
>>*God shall lift up thy head.*
>
>*Through waves, and clouds, and storms,*
>>*He gently clears thy way;*
>*Wait thou his time – thy darkest night*
>>*Shall end in brightest day.*

Remember that this casting of our care on God is a present and a constant duty. It is in the form of the present tense that the Holy Ghost, the Comforter, addresses us: 'Casting all your care upon him.' Defer it not until the morrow, nor wait a better frame. Do it now! A present care will find a present Receiver, a present Helper, and a present relief. The Lord your God neither accepts nor rejects, grants nor denies you, because of the high or the low frame with which you approach him. To suppose that the spiritual tone of your mind influenced his decision, would be to make the turning-point of his love to centre in you rather than in himself and to argue that God was moved by other motives than those found within his own heart. God's dealings with us from first to last, in the greatest and in the least, from the love that chose us from everlasting to the smile that sheds its bright halo around our dying pillow, proceed from the principle of his most free grace. And since he finds the motive of love and the bestowment of blessing solely within himself, he, the unchangeable One, will not revoke the love nor withdraw the gift influenced by any fickleness or change he traces in you. Then, be your frame low, your heart dead, your faith weak, arise and draw near to God, for the blood-tipped sceptre bids you approach and the blessing, the richest God can bestow or you desire, awaits your full acceptance.

Oh yes, the Lord cares for *you*! Little, obscure, despised, unworthy though you may be or deem yourself to be, the Lord has an interest in you, the closest, the tenderest that ever dwelt in a heart of love. Bought with the Saviour's blood, a temple of the Holy Ghost, sealed with the earnest of the Spirit as a child of God and an heir of glory, oh, there is not a bright angel in heaven for whom God so cares as he cares for you! Will you not respond to this truth by transferring all your care to him in the exercise of a humble, unquestioning faith? Others may have ceased to care for you. Change has congealed the warm current of love, distance intercepts its flow, or death has stilled its pulse, and you feel as if there existed in this wide world no heart, no spirit, no mind that responded to, or that chimed and blended with your own. Yes; there is One! Jesus cares for you. The heart of God, from which all other hearts kindle their affection, entwines you with its thoughts, its sympathies, its love; and the eye that searches the universe with a glance, bends upon you its ceaseless look of love. 'When my father and my mother forsake me', when human affection departs from its last, its latest, its most sacred home on earth, 'then the LORD will take me up' (*Psa.* 27:10). The desolateness of widowhood shall claim his sympathy, the friendlessness of being orphaned shall receive his protection, the suffering and languor of sickness shall be sustained by his grace, the grief of bereavement shall be soothed by his love, and the bed and valley of death shall be cheered and brightened with his radiant presence.

Then, confide in and lean upon this divine, this human, this precious, this ever-present Saviour. He asks your boundless confidence and your warmest love. He is most worthy of it. Will you withhold it? Take that anxious care which lies like lead upon your breast, which chases peace from your mind, joy from your heart, slumber from your pillow, shading all the landscape of life with wintry frost and storm, and lay it upon the heart pierced by the soldier's lance, the heart that distilled its last drop of life-blood on the tree, and peace shall enfold you beneath its balmy wing. 'Be careful for nothing; but in every thing by prayer and supplication with thanksgiving let your requests be made known unto God. And the peace of God, which passeth all understanding, shall keep your hearts and minds through Christ Jesus' (*Phil.* 4:6–7).

Shall I not trust my God,
  Who doth so well love me –
Who, as a Father, cares so tenderly?
  Shall I not lay the load
Which would my weakness break,
  On his strong hand, who never doth forsake?

He doth know all my grief,
  And all my heart's desire;
He'll stand by me till death, through flood and fire.
  And he can send relief:
My Father's love, so free,
  Till the new morning shall remain to me.

Who doth the birds supply,
  Who grass, and trees, and flowers,
Doth beautifully clothe, through ceaseless hours;
  Who hears us ere we cry;
Can he my need forget?
  Nay, though he slay me, I will trust him yet.

When I his yoke do bear,
  And seek my chiefest joy
But in his righteousness and sweet employ:
  He makes my soul his care;
Early and late doth bless,
  And crowneth work and purpose with success.

O blessed be his name!
  My Father cares for me!
I can no longer unbelieving be;
  All praise to him proclaim;
I know he is my Friend –
  I know the Lord will love me to the end!

CHAPTER 8

Self-Communion

Commune with your own heart upon your
bed, and be still.
— Psalm 4:4

It will be acknowledged by every spiritual and reflecting mind that the tendencies of the age are not the most favourable to the calm, solemn, holy duty of self-communion. We are fallen upon times of great religious as well as worldly activity and excitement. So strong and rushing indeed is the tide, that there exists a fearful and fatal liability in those who profess to walk with God, as did Noah and Enoch, to neglect entirely one of the most essential and effectual helps heavenward – the due, faithful, and constant examination of the spiritual state and condition of their own hearts. To the consideration of this vitally important subject, a subject so intimately entwined with our progress in the divine life, let us now address ourselves. The divine precept is emphatic: 'Commune with your own heart upon your bed, and be still.' 'Come, my people, enter thou into thy chambers' (*Isa.* 26:20), is the invitation of God to his church. Similar to this is the Saviour's exhortation, "When thou prayest, enter into thy closet" (*Matt.* 6:6).

The great mass of human beings by whom we are surrounded are in the closest communion with everything but themselves. Man is in communion with nature in its glories, with science in its wonders, with art in its triumphs, with intellect in its attainments, with power in its achievements, with the creation in its attraction. There is but one object with which he holds no rational, sacred, and close communion, and from which, though the nearest and the most important, he seems the most widely isolated; that object is himself. He studies not the wonders of his being, the spirituality of his nature, the solemnity of his relations, the accountability of his actions, the immortality of his destiny. He thinks not of himself, and death, and judgment, and eternity at the same moment. He will examine and prepare himself for worldly preferment, but his state as a moral being, his position as a responsible being, his future as an accountable and deathless being, absorbs not a moment, awakens not a thought, inspires not an aspiration of his soul. What a fearful verification of and comment upon the Word of God, 'dead in trespasses and in sins'!

But the saints of God present another and a widely different class. The religion of Jesus, while it is designed to disarm man of selfishness and, when enthroned supremely upon the heart, ennobles and expands it with the 'expulsive power of a new affection', yet concentrates his most serious, devout, and earnest consideration upon himself. 'Man, know thyself,' a heathen maxim, becomes in its highest and noblest sense, Christianized. It is of the utmost importance, then, that the saint of God should be kept in perpetual remembrance of this sacred duty of self-communion; its neglect entails immense spiritual deterioration and loss; its observance will, more than all other engagements – for it stimulates to activity all others – effectually advance the soul in its heavenward course. Self-communion is the topic which will now engage our thoughts – may we give to it the devout and earnest consideration which a subject so closely intertwined with our personal advance in heavenly meetness demands. Oh, that this chapter of our work may be written and read under the special anointing of God the Holy Ghost! Let us endeavour to ascertain what this sacred duty involves.

In the first place, my beloved reader, commune with your own heart, to know its true spiritual state as before God. This will bring under your review the subject of conversion, a state which many take for granted without scriptural evidence of the fact; a great matter in which too many assume the existence of their personal conversion without proof. And yet how vast the consequences of the most momentous question they take for granted! There is no statement clearer in God's Word than this, that to enjoy heaven we must become heavenly. God cannot cease to be God; therefore he could not make us, like himself, perfectly happy, unless he made us, like himself, perfectly holy. The Holy Ghost must make us new creatures, the subjects of a nature that is divine, in order to fit us for the enjoyment of a heaven that is pure. The questions, then, which we must weigh are: Have I passed from death unto life? Has my heart been convinced of sin? Am I a subject of the new birth? From a state of insensibility to objects, and feelings, and hopes that are spiritual, eternal, and divine, have I been quickened by the regenerating Spirit to walk with God and before the world in newness of life? These are personal and serious questions, which must not, which cannot, be

evaded without imperilling all that is most dear and precious to your everlasting well-being.

Oh, give to your eyes no slumber until the subject of
the new birth has awakened in your mind the profoundest thought! It is spoken by him who is the Truth, and it
is written by him who is the Spirit of Truth, 'Except a
man be born again, he cannot see the kingdom of God'
(*John* 3:3). Heaven or hell is suspended upon the issue!
My reader, are you aware that within you all things have
been made new; that, whereas once you were blind,
now you see; that your heart is in sympathy with objects
that are spiritual, with enjoyments that are holy, with
engagements that are heavenly? In a word, are you sensible that your views of sin and self, of God and of Christ
and of the gospel, are radically, essentially changed, and
that you seem to yourself the subject of a new-born existence and the occupant of a new-created world?

Commune with yourself to ascertain the existence
and condition of the love of God in your heart. Enmity
or love to Jehovah characterises us; there is no modified
state between these extremes. A careful inspection of our
hearts as to this principle will enable us correctly to decide our spiritual condition before the Lord. Do you love
God because he is holy; his law, because it is righteous;
his government, because it is divine and just; his ways,
because they are wise, and right, and sure? Do you love
him for sending his Son into the world to save sinners?
Do you love him as a Father, as a Friend, as a God in
covenant relation? How stands your heart, oh believer,
with God as to its love? What is the warmth and vigour
and ardour of your affections? Do you so love God in
Christ as, under its constraining influence, to do what he
commands, to yield what he asks, to go where he bids,

to hate what he hates, and to love what he loves; yea, to embrace him with an affection simple, single, and supreme, oblivious, if need be, of every other claimant, and satisfied, if so he willed it, with him alone?

Oh, what is the state of your love to Jesus – frigid, selfish, inconstant; or glowing, self-denying, fixed? You ask how your love to Christ may be tested and increased? Test it by obedience; 'If ye love me, keep my commandments' (*John* 14:15). Increase it by a more close, believing dealing with Christ's love to you. Your love to Christ will never increase by feeding upon itself. You must light your torch of affection at the altar of Calvary. You must go there, and learn and believe what the love of Jesus is to you: the vastness of that love, the self-sacrifice of that love, how that love of Christ laboured and wept, bled, suffered, and died for you. Can you stand before this love, this love so precious, so great, so enduring, so self-consuming, so changeless, and know that for you was this offering, for you this cross, for you this agony, for you this scorn and insult, for you this death, and feel no sensibility, no emotion, no love? Impossible! Sit not down, then, in vain regrets that your love to God in Christ is so frigid, so fickle, so dubious; go and muse upon the reality, the greatness, the present intercession of the Saviour's love to you, and if love can inspire love, then I think that, while you muse, the fire will burn and your soul shall be all aflame with love to God. 'The Lord direct your hearts into the love of God' (2 *Thess.* 3:5).

> *Were the whole realm of nature mine,*
> *That were a present far too small;*
> *Love so amazing, so divine,*
> *Demands my soul, my life, my all.*

Commune with your own heart as to its views of, and its feelings towards, the Lord Jesus. The great question which decides so much is, 'What think ye of Christ?' (*Matt.* 22:42). Is it with you a reality that Christ died for sinners? Do you fully credit the promise by which God has engaged to accept through his sacrifice and intercession all who believe in his name? Do you believe him to be divine, accept his obedience as justifying and his death as sacrificial? Has it pleased God to reveal his Son in you? Is he precious to your heart? And do you receive him, trust in him, follow him, and hope to be with him forever, as all your salvation and all your desire?

You ask me how you may come to a right conclusion in the matter. You long, you yearn, you pray to know whether or not you love Christ, are one of his disciples, and shall certainly be with him where he is. But why doubt it? Is the matter so difficult? If your mind were filled with admiration of a being, could you question the emotion thus awakened? If your heart were captivated by an object of superior intellect and beauty, and that object towards which the yearning and clinging of your affection went forth in a warm and ceaseless flow, became supremely enthroned in your sympathy and regard, would the fact admit of a moment's doubt? Would you call in question the existence, the reality, or even the intensity of your love? Impossible! The higher and more momentous question of your attachment to Christ admits of a yet easier solution. Do I love Jesus? Is he the object of my supreme admiration and delight? Is he the chosen, the preferred, the supreme Being of my warmest affection? Is he precious to my soul? And am I trusting believingly, and exclusively, and without mental reservation, as a sinner utterly undone, self-abhorred, and self-condemned, to his atoning sacrifice? And still you hesitate! And yet you doubt! It is still a problem which you tremble to solve. You think of your sinfulness, your unworthiness, of the taint and flaw and unloveliness of all you are doing, of your faint love, of your weak faith, of your doubtful sincerity, and then you shrink from the thought of claiming an interest in Christ and resign yourself to the conviction that your salvation is an utter impossibility, that you are not, and never will be, saved!

But let us take a closer view of the matter. Upon what ground do you base this hesitation and justify this self-exemption from the great salvation? It is not for your worth that you are saved, but for Christ's worth. It is not on the ground of your personal merits that you are justified, but on the ground of Christ's merits alone. It is not upon the plea of your fitness, your tears, your confessions, your prayers, your duties, that God forgives and accepts you, but simply and exclusively upon the one plea of the Saviour's sacrifice. The blood of Christ pardons, the righteousness of Christ justifies you, and this is all that you require, or that God demands. The great work is all done – it is not to *be* done. It is complete, finished, accepted, sealed. And you, as a lost sinner, without holiness, without strength, without one plea that springs from what you are, have nothing to do. Believe, and you are saved. Believing is not doing, it is not meriting. It is trusting, it is the simple exercise of a faith in Christ which God gives and which the Holy Ghost produces in the heart; so that your salvation, from beginning to end, is entirely out of yourself, in another.

With what clearness and emphasis has the Spirit of truth set this forth: 'By the works of the law shall no flesh be justified' (*Gal.* 2:16), 'but to him that worketh

not, but believeth on him that justifieth the ungodly, his
faith is counted for righteousness' (*Rom.* 4:5). All your
own works, until your faith embraces the Lord Jesus, are
'dead works', and dead works never took a soul to
heaven. You need as much the atoning blood to purge
you from dead works as to purge you from deadly sins.
Hear the words of the Holy Ghost: 'How much more
shall the blood of Christ, who through the eternal Spirit
offered himself without spot to God, purge your conscience from dead works to serve the living God?' (*Heb.*
9:14). And do you still ask, 'What then must I *do* to be
saved?' Do! I answer – nothing! All is done, completely
and for ever done! Blessed, oh thrice blessed be God!
Christ has done it all, paid it all, endured it all, suffered it
all, finished it all, leaving you, O sin-burdened, anxious,
trembling, hesitating soul, nothing to do, and only to believe. Will not this suffice? Will you demur a moment
longer to commit yourself to Christ, to lay your soul on
Jesus, to accept the salvation, the heaven, the crown, the
eternal life he proffers you as the free bestowments of
his grace? Your sins, countless as the stars, are no barrier
to your salvation if you but believe in Jesus. Your transgressions, deep as scarlet and as crimson, shall not be of
too deep a dye if you but plunge into the fountain of
Christ's blood. His delight, his glory is to receive sinners,
to receive you. And the moment you cease to give over
doing, and begin only to believe, from that moment
your soul rests from its labour, you enter into peace, and
are for ever saved!

> *Nothing, either great or small,*
>   *Nothing, sinner, no;*
> *Jesus did it, did it all,*
>   *Long, long ago.*

When he from his lofty throne
  Stoop'd to do and die,
Everything was fully done;
  Hearken to his cry –

'It is finish'd!' Yes indeed,
  Finish'd every jot.
Sinner, this is all you need;
  Tell me, is it not?

Weary, working, burden'd one,
  Why do you toil so?
Cease your doing; all was done
  Long, long ago.

Till to Jesus' work you cling
  By a simple faith,
'Doing' is a deadly thing –
  'Doing' ends in death.

Cast your deadly 'doing' down –
  Down at Jesus' feet;
Stand 'in him,' in him alone,
  Gloriously complete!

Commune with your own heart touching its ruling principles of action. It is a law of our moral being that the human heart must be governed by some all-controlling, all-commanding principle, some secret potent spring that moves and regulates the entire powers of the soul. What is the ruling principle of your heart? Have you examined yourself to know? Beware of self-treachery, the most easy and the most fatal of all species of deception. There are many deceitful things in the world. The wind is deceitful, the ocean is deceitful, the creature is deceitful, but the human 'heart is deceitful above all things' (Jer. 17:9), and in nothing, probably,

more so than in the principles and motives which govern and sway it. Oh, it is appalling to think what
self-idolatry and self-seeking and self-complacence may
reign in our hearts, prompt and govern our actions!
How carefully and nicely may we adjust our sail and
shape our course to catch the soft breath and win the
low murmur of man's approbation and acclaim as we
float on the bosom of the stream, while ostensibly we are
doing all for God!

But, retreating to my chamber, let me, in solitude,
self-scrutiny, and prayer, commune with my own heart.
Laying bare, as with the deepest incision of the knife, its
spiritual anatomy before God, my motives, purposes,
and aims, can I say, 'Lord, sinful though I am, the chief
of sinners, yet do I desire to be ruled in my life by thy
Word, to be governed in my principles by thy fear, to be
constrained in thy service by thy love, and to make thy
honour and glory the end of all I do'? Thus ruled and
swayed, how fragrant and acceptable to him your lowliest service, your humblest offering! It may be but the
'widow's mite' you have cast into the treasury, to him it
is more costly than the jewelled diadem. It may be but a
'cup of cold water' you have offered to a disciple in his
name, to him it is as beautiful and sparkling as the crystal river which flows from beneath his throne. It may be
a service for Christ you have done, imperfect in itself
and trying to your spirit, unrecognized and unrewarded
by others; yet the tribute of your heart, in harmony with
his will and promotive of his glory, this box of precious
ointment which you have broken shall fill earth with the
fragrance of your love, and heaven with the music of
Christ's praise.

Commune with your own heart, and ascertain its

heavenly tendencies – whether the shadow of time or the realities of eternity have the ascendancy. Let no child of God deem such a scrutiny needless. The Word of God is replete with exhortations to the church to set its affections on things above and not on the earth; to seek first the kingdom of God; to have its conversation in heaven. Encompassed as we are by earth, blinded by objects of sense, weighed down by human cares and anxieties, we need to be watchful against their secular influence upon our minds. It is good, therefore, to retire to our chamber and examine the spiritual barometer of the soul, to adjust the balance of the affections, and to see that divine and eternal realities are obtaining a growing ascendency and pre-eminence. How distinct and impressive the precept, 'Love not the world, neither the things that are in the world. If any man love the world, the love of the Father is not in him' (1 John 2:15). 'Be not conformed to this world: but be ye transformed' (Rom. 12:2). 'Who gave himself for our sins, that he might deliver us from this present evil world, according to the will of God and our Father' (Gal. 1:4).

Commune with your own heart as to its real and habitual fellowship with God. Do we pray? What is the character of our prayers? Do we pray in the Spirit? Do we commune in prayer? Do we walk with God as a Father, and with Christ as our best Friend? And is the throne of grace the sweetest, holiest, dearest spot to us on earth? For the lack of this honest communion with our heart, there is often an essential defect in our communion with the heart of Jesus. Our hearts grow so cold that we are insensible to the warmth of his. There is so little self-examination touching prayer, that our devotions glide into a cold, abstract formality, and petitions and suppli-

cations which should be as swift arrows shot from the
bow of faith entering into the presence of God, congeal
as icicles upon our lips. Oh, look well to the state of your
heart in the matter of prayer; it is the true, the safest test
of the spiritual condition of your soul! See that your devotions are the utterances of the Spirit, sprinkled with
atoning blood and offered in the lowly, loving spirit of
adoption, the breathing of a child to God as your Father.
This is 'fellowship', and all other is but the name.

Commune with your own heart as to your progress
in the divine life. It is impossible to know correctly the
distance we are on our heavenward way, the stages we
have travelled, the points we have reached, without
self-communion. The mariner examines his ocean-chart,
the traveller the milestones of the road, to mark the
progress he has made homewards; how much more necessary this for the voyager to eternity, for the traveller to
the heavenly Zion! Everything in nature is advancing –
nothing is stationary. Progress is the universal law of the
universe. Is the renewed soul, the heavenly traveller,
alone to stand still? Is the living water, stored within the
soul of the regenerate, alone to be stagnant? Is the kingdom of grace alone exempt from the operation of this
law of progress? Let your inquiry then be, how high is
my sun in the moral heavens? How near is it to its glorious setting? How far am I from the haven whither my
soul longeth to be, sheltered from storm and billow in
eternal safety and repose? 'Knowing the time, that now
it is high time to awake out of sleep: for now is our salvation nearer than when we believed' (*Rom.* 13:11).

And, then, as to the dealings of our heavenly Father,
how close should be our self-communion! God deals
with us that we might deal with ourselves, and then

with him. An affliction often recalls our thoughts and sympathies and care from others and concentrates them upon our more neglected self. 'They made me the keeper of the vineyards; but mine own vineyard have I not kept' (*Song of Sol.* 1:6). Why has the Lord, perhaps, taken you apart from the activities of life, from the duties of your family, and from the religious engagements which have been so exciting and absorbing? Just that in this lone hour, in this quiet chamber, on this bed of sickness and reflection, you might be the better schooled in the much neglected duty of self-communion.

God would have you now ascertain the why and the wherefore of this present discipline: what backsliding this stroke is to correct; what sin this chastening is to chide; what declension this probing is to discover; what neglected duty this rebuke is to make known; what disobeyed command this rod is to reveal. Oh, how needed and wholesome and precious is self-communion now! Never before, perhaps, has your heart been laid open to such inspection, subjected to such scrutiny, submitted to such tests. Never have you been brought into such close contact with yourself; never has self-communion appeared to you so needed, so solemn, and so blessed as in this quiet chamber. Ah, much abused, much neglected heart, how have I allowed thee to wander, to be enamoured, enchained, won, and possessed by others! How has thy spiritual verdure withered, how have thy fresh springs dried, thy beauty faded, and thy strength decayed! How cold, how inconstant, how unfaithful, how unkind hast thou been to thy best, thy dearest, thy heavenly Friend! If it were not for the restraints of his grace, and the constraints of his love, and the checks of his gentle corrections, whither, oh, whither wouldst thou have gone? I thank thee, Lord, for thy discipline, for the shaded path, the severed tie, the lonely sorrow, the loving, lenient correction that recalls my heart to thee!

Commune with your own heart to ascertain its state touching the existence and exercise of the spirit of thanksgiving and praise. There is scarcely any part of our religious experience that receives less attention and insight than this. And in consequence of its neglect, we lose much personal holiness, and God much glory. Praise is as much an element of our Christianity, as distinctly a duty and a privilege, as prayer. And yet how little of it do we exhibit! We are so absorbed by the trials and discouragements of the Christian pilgrimage as to overlook its blessings and its helps. We dwell so much upon the sombre colouring of the daily picture of life as to be insensible to its brighter hues. But did we deal more with the good and less with the evil; did we weigh our mercies with our trials; were we to reflect that if one sorrow is sent, how much heavier a sorrow that one may have prevented; if one trial comes, how much greater that trial might have been, and that when the Lord sends us one discomfort or permits one reverse, he sends us many comforts and crowns our arms with many victories; that there is not a dispensation of his providence, whatever its form and complexion, that is not a vehicle of mercy, that does not breathe a beatitude; that the blessing of God, the smile of Jesus, and the voice of the Spirit's love, are in every event and incident and circumstance of our history, then, what a more thankful, praiseful spirit should we cherish!

How should we examine our hearts to discover and expel thence the lurking spirit of murmur and rebellion and fretting against the Lord! How should we uplift every window and remove every veil that would limit the beams of God's goodness entering and penetrating every recess, lighting up the entire soul with the sunshine of mercy, and making it vocal with the music of praise! I have exhorted you, beloved reader, to cultivate self-communion as to the matter of prayer; with equal point and earnestness do I exhort you to this holy duty as to the matter of praise. There exists a serious defect in the Christianity, a sad lack in the religious experience, of many of the Lord's people touching this holy exercise. The Lord has declared, 'Whoso offereth praise glorifieth me' (*Psa.* 50:23). And the holy apostle, speaking by the Spirit, exhorts, 'Be careful for nothing; but in every thing by prayer and supplication with thanksgiving let your requests be made known unto God' (*Phil.* 4:6). And in another place we learn how comprehensive is this precept, 'Giving thanks always for all things unto God and the Father in the name of our Lord Jesus Christ' (*Eph.* 5:20). Thanks always for *all* things!

So then I am to cultivate a feeling of gratitude and to breathe a spirit of praise for all that my God and Father pleases to send me. I am always to be in a thankful, praising spirit for all the dispensations of his providence and grace. What a holy state will my soul then be in! What happiness it will ensure to my heart, and what a revenue of glory will accrue to God! How it will lighten my burdens, soothe my cares, heal the chafings of sorrow, and shed beams of sunshine upon many a lonely, dreary stage of my journey. I praise too little. I look only to the crossing of my will, to the disappointment of my hopes, to the foil of my plans, to what my Father sees fit to restrain and withhold, and not to the mercies and blessings, bright as the stars which glow and chime above me and numerous as the sand of the ocean upon which in pensive sadness I tread; therefore it is that while those stars chant his praise and those sands speak his goodness and power, I alone am silent! And yet, my Father, there is nothing in thyself nor in thy dealings which ought not to inspire my deepest gratitude and praise to thee!

> *I thank thee, O my God, who made*
>   *The earth so bright;*
> *So full of splendour and of joy,*
>   *Beauty and light;*
> *So many glorious things are here,*
>   *Noble and right!*
>
> *I thank thee, too, that thou hast made*
>   *Joy to abound;*
> *So many gentle thoughts and deeds*
>   *Circling us round,*
> *That in the darkest spot on earth*
>   *Some love is found.*
>
> *I thank thee more that all our joy*
>   *Is touch'd with pain;*
> *That shadows fall on brightest hours;*
>   *That thorns remain;*
> *So that earth's bliss may be our guide,*
>   *And not our chain.*
>
> *For thou who knowest, Lord, how soon*
>   *Our weak heart clings,*
> *Hast given us joys, tender and true,*
>   *Yet all with wings,*
> *So that we see, gleaming on high,*
>   *Diviner things!*
>
> *I thank thee, Lord, that thou hast kept*
>   *The best in store;*

We have enough, yet not too much
  To wish for more;
A yearning for a deeper peace,
  Not known before.

I thank thee, Lord, that here our souls,
  Though amply blest,
Can never find, although they seek,
  A perfect rest;
Nor ever shall, until they lean
  On Jesus' breast!
— Proctor

If, my beloved reader, there is one caution which I would urge with deeper emphasis of meaning and solemnity of spirit than another, it is this – be not satisfied without the clearest evidence of the personal possession of heart religion. In nothing does there exist a greater tendency, a more easy road to fatal self-destruction than in this. The substitutes for heart-religion are so many and subtle that without the closest scrutiny and the most rigid analysis of religious feeling and action, we may be betrayed, unsuspectingly to ourselves, into the gravest error. You may be religious, very religious, conscientiously religious, and yet be destitute of vital religion. Denominational partisanship is not religion. Religious activity is not religion. You may be the warm promoter and patron of that which is Christian and philanthropic and useful in its nature – the school, the hospital, the market, the society – and yet not possess religion! You may aid in the building of churches, in the appointment of ministers, in the securing of endowments, in the sanitary, moral, and intellectual well-being of a community, and still be destitute of vital religion. You may submit to the rite of baptism, may go to the Lord's table, may take upon you in any form the vows of God, and yet remain without a changed heart and a renewed mind. All this which I have been describing is still-life of a religious kind, the mere galvanism, the simulation, the counterfeit of vital godliness, a wretched copy of the original. Examine yourself by these tests: Do I know that my sins are pardoned through Christ? Have I peace with God in Jesus? Am I living in the enjoyment of the Spirit of adoption? Have I in my soul the happiness, the joy, the consolation, the hope which heart-religion imparts? Or, solemn thought, am I endeavoring to quiet my conscience, to stifle self-reflection, to divert my thoughts from my unsatisfactory, unhappy condition and state of mind by the religious substitutes and subterfuges with which the present age so profusely abounds and which, with those who are ensnared by them, pass for real spiritual life? Oh, commune faithfully with your own heart touching this matter!

A few directions as to the manner of engaging in this solemn duty of self-communion:

For a spiritual work, we must, in its engagement, seek earnestly the aid of the Holy Spirit. He alone can enable us to unlock the wards, to unravel the mystery, and to penetrate into the veiled depths of our own heart. We need the knowledge, the grace, the love of the Spirit in a task so purely spiritual as this. Let us, then, betake ourselves to the Holy Ghost, invoke his power, supplicate his grace, and seek his renewed anointing. Enshrined in our hearts, his newly created and perpetual home, he is better acquainted with them than we are ourselves and is prepared to aid us faithfully and successfully to discharge this difficult and humbling task of self-communion. 'Ye have an unction from the Holy One, and ye know all things' (*1 John* 2:20). This divine anointing will essentially assist you in an experimental knowledge of yourself.

Blend communion with Christ with self-communion. Let converse with your own heart be in unison with converse with the heart of God. Endeavour to realize that in this sacred engagement God is with you, his thoughts towards you are thoughts of peace, and the feelings of his heart are the warm pulsations of his love. Associate all views of yourself with this view of God: that whatever discoveries you arrive at of waywardness and folly, idolatry and sin, however dark and humiliating the inward picture, not a frown of displeasure shall glance from his eye, nor a word of reproach breathe from his lips. Oh do you think that he will join in your self-accusation, that because you loathe, and abhor, and condemn yourself, he will likewise loathe, abhor, and condemn you? Never. Listen to his words: 'Thus saith the high and lofty One that inhabiteth eternity, whose name is Holy; I dwell in the high and holy place, with him also that is of a contrite and humble spirit, to revive the spirit of the humble, and to revive the heart of the contrite ones' (*Isa.* 57:15). Bending low at his feet in penitential acknowledgment of sin, in the holy act of self-communion and prayer, no atmosphere shall encircle and embrace you but the atmosphere of divine forgiving love.

I venture to suggest another and the most important direction in this work of self-communion: commune with your own heart, looking fully to the cross of Christ. Without this, self-examination may induce the spirit of bondage. It should never be entered upon but upon the principles and in the spirit of the gospel. It is only as we deal closely with the atonement, we can deal closely with sin. It is only as we deal faithfully with the blood that we can deal faithfully with our own hearts. Overwhelming were the revelations of a rigid self-scrutiny except for the hold faith maintains of the sacrifice of Christ and the close, realizing apprehension it has of the cross of Jesus. You must commune with Christ's heart and your own heart at the same moment! Looking at Jesus in the face, you will be enabled to look your sins in the face; and as your love to him deepens, so will deepen your self-abhorrence for sin. As has been beautifully remarked, 'for one look at yourself, take ten looks at Christ'; no dark discovery will then sink you to despair.

Ah, how little we deal with the heart of our Lord! We find finite depths of iniquity in our own, but we forget the infinite depths of grace that are in his. Ours is cold and fickle in its love and constancy, his is overflowing with a love as changeless and immutable as his being. Oh, then, take every discovery you make in this humbling task of self-scrutiny to Christ. Remember that if you are a believer in the Lord Jesus, every sin and infirmity and deficiency you discover, Christ has died for, he has shed his blood for and has for ever put away; and that, repairing anew to his atonement and his grace, you shall have your iniquities subdued, and your conscience purified, and your soul reinstated in a sense of pardon and divine acceptance. It is beneath the cross alone that sin shall be seen, hated, conquered, and forsaken. Sin, guilt, unbelief, and impenitence cannot live a moment under the sacred shadow of the cross of Christ. Drag your foe there, and it is slain. Go there, my soul, and weep, mourn, and love; and in communing with thine

own heart, oh, forget not the yet deeper, closer communion with the heart of Jesus!

We will group together a few of the hallowed blessings that result from this habit of self-communion. In the
first place, it will help to keep you acquainted with the
true state of your soul. By this daily survey you will
know how matters stand between God and your own
conscience. Sin shall not seek supremacy, and you not
know it; the world will not obtain an ascendancy, and
you not be conscious of it; the creature will not become
idolatrous, and you not be suspicious of its encroachment; Christ will not grow less in your estimation and
love, and you remain insensible to the change. Self-
communion will keep you whole nights upon your
watch-tower, and the foe shall not surprise you.

The duty, too, will increasingly deepen the conviction of your individuality. You will feel it to be a solemn
privilege to commune with your own heart; and thus
your own responsibility – a fact so lamentably overlooked
– will appear in its proper and impressive light. How few
indulge in this searching inquiry into the state of their
own hearts, lest their self-esteem should be lowered!
Hence it is that we meet continually with persons possessed of great shrewdness and sagacity in all other
matters who are most lamentably ignorant of themselves. Many have obtained an extraordinary knowledge
of mankind in general and can discover at once the
weak points of every individual, but are pitiably blind to
every one of their own infirmities. It is amusing to observe that of all persons within the circle of their
acquaintanceship they are perhaps the only parties to
whom their own failings are unknown.

Then, prosecuting honestly and vigorously this self-research, you will have less time and still less inclination to examine and judge your fellows. Vain and officious attempts to penetrate and unveil the hearts of others will give place to the yet more neglected, important, and humbling work of examining, unveiling, and searching your own heart. Oh, that all who profess the name of the Lord Jesus were more deeply concerned about the spiritual condition of themselves as in the sight of God! There would then be less censoriousness and uncharitableness, less judging the motives and condemning the actions of others, and more humility, kindness, and love in the Church of God. Commune with your own heart, and leave to others the solemn responsibility and duty of communing with theirs. To their Master they stand or fall. Enter into your chamber, and in the solemn, the awful stillness of an hour spent alone with God, deal with your own heart and be still. This work faithfully done, you will emerge thence too much filled with astonishment and condemnation at the discoveries you have made of your own self, to examine, judge, and condemn others!

Self-communion, too, will greatly conduce to growth in personal holiness. The eye will be more concentrated upon the seat of evil, the sentinel of your heart will be more wakeful, and sin and temptation will have less power to surprise and overcome you. It will also promote true humility. Self-communion will lead to self acquaintance, and this in its turn will dispel those vain delusions and conceits with which the flattery of others may have inflated us. Alas that there should be so much religious flattery and complimenting – the most ensnaring and injurious of all species of adulation – among professors of religion! Here is the antidote – self-knowledge. This will turn the fine edge of the fatal weapon – self-communion.

The too fond and partial opinion of your graces, your spiritual attainments and your usefulness, expressed by others, will leave you unscathed if you are found in much communion with your own heart in your chamber. Few spiritual engagements, too, will more vigorously promote in your soul the yet higher and more solemn one of prayer. To know in some degree ourselves – the heart, whose infirmities others see not, nor even suspect, but which we know to be so vile – is to compel us to prayer.

Once more, how precious will Jesus grow with growing self-communion. How will it endear his atonement, his grace, yea, himself, to the heart! That engagement which deepens the conviction of our own sinfulness, helplessness, and need, which discovers to us taint and flaw and imperfection in the 'hidden part', the fountain all poisoned and impure, must deepen our sense of the infinite worth and preciousness of the Saviour. Whither can we look with one gleam of hope but to his blood and righteousness? That sacrifice offered once for all, that divine atonement, that perfect work, that righteousness that raises us above all demerit into the sunshine of God's presence, the light of which reveals not a speck upon us, just meets our case, quells our fears, and assures us of divine acceptance. Surely, then, the closer the acquaintance we form with ourselves, whilst it throws us upon the Saviour, must render him an object increasingly precious to our hearts.

Dealing closely with our own selves in the time of God's dispensations will elucidate much that is obscure, explain much that is mysterious, and soothe much that is painful and sad. When the psalmist was sorely tried in his soul, when his sore ran in the night and ceased not, when his soul refused to be comforted and his spirit was overwhelmed, when he was so troubled that he could not speak, then came the remedy: 'I call to remembrance my song in the night: I commune with mine own heart: and my spirit made diligent search' (*Psa.* 77:6). And when he arose from this process of self-communion, searching into all the thousand memories of God's past lovingkindness and faithfulness laid up in the heart, he was a victor over all his dark forebodings, and gloomy fears, and depressing sorrows; his faith confirmed in the truth that the Lord never casts off his people, that his promise fails not for evermore, that he had not forgotten to be gracious, nor in anger had shut up his tender mercies.

Is thy heart searching for one spring of comfort, for one ray of hope, for one throb of love in this the long, dreary night of thy sorrow? Search, O child of God, for thou shalt find some stored remembrance there of God's past faithfulness and love, and this shall be a token to thee that all that the Lord thy God has been to thee, he is now and will be forever. 'When my heart is over-whelmed: lead me to the rock that is higher than I' (*Psa.* 61:2). 'Be still!' Let communion with your own heart soothe it to perfect peace and repose, calm in the assurance that nothing shall separate it from God's love, that the government of all worlds and all beings and all things is upon Christ's shoulders, that your heavenly Father is causing all things in your individual history to work together for good, and that you may wait with confidence, quietness, and cheerful composure the issue of the night of gloom and tears which now enshrouds your soul within its gloomy pavilion. 'Search me, O God, and know my heart: try me, and know my thoughts:

and see if there be any wicked way in me, and lead me
in the way everlasting' (*Psa.* 139:23–24).

> *And what am I? My soul awake,*
> *And an impartial survey take;*
> *Does no dark sign, no ground of fear,*
> *In practice or in heart appear?*
>
> *What image does my spirit bear?*
> *Is Jesus form'd and living there?*
> *Say, do his lineaments divine*
> *In thought, in word, and action shine?*
>
> *Searcher of hearts! oh, search me still;*
> *The secrets of my soul reveal;*
> *My fears remove, let me appear*
> *To God and my own conscience clear!*
>
> *Scatter the clouds which o'er my head*
> *Thick glooms of dubious terrors spread;*
> *Lead me into celestial day,*
> *And to myself, myself display.*
>
> *May I at that blest world arrive*
> *Where Christ through all my soul shall live,*
> *And give full proof that he is there,*
> *Without one gloomy doubt or fear!*

CHAPTER 9

Backsliders Returning

Return, ye backsliding children, and I will heal your backslidings. Behold, we come unto thee; for thou art the LORD our God.

— Jeremiah 3:22

There are some unveilings of God's heart which can only be understood and met by responsive unfoldings of ours. It is not the flinty, impervious rock that welcomes and absorbs the heaven-distilling dew. Upon such an object in nature, beautiful and grand though it may be, the life-quickening moisture, thus descending, is a thankless and fruitless offering, a useless expenditure of one of nature's richest treasures. But let that dew, noiseless and unseen, fall upon the flower, the herb, the tree, the earth which the ploughshare has upturned and the furrow has broken, and how refreshing the boon, and how rich the return! Thus is it with such an exhibition of the heart of God as that which we have just presented, inimitable in its tenderness, unsurpassed in its condescension and grace. Let those words distil upon any other than a heart humbled, softened, lying low in a low place, in the consciousness of its sinful departure, its sad backsliding from God, and they awake no tender, holy, grateful response.

But how beautiful are the reciprocal influences of the human and the divine as presented in the narrative! 'A voice was heard upon the high places, weeping and supplications of the children of Israel: for they have perverted their way, and they have forgotten the LORD their God' (*Jer.* 3:21). That voice of weeping entered into the ears of God, and behold the gracious invitation: 'Return, ye backsliding children, and I will heal your backslidings' (*Jer.* 3:22). And then follows the instant and grateful response: 'Behold, we come unto thee; for thou art the LORD our God' (*Jer.* 3:22). Mark how divine and restoring grace gently falls upon the lowly, penitent, returning soul; and then how the sin-contrite heart of the child goes forth to meet and embrace the sin-forgiving heart of the Father. Few will read the pages of a work designed to proffer a helping hand to Zion's travellers to whom that hand will be more needful and acceptable than the awakened, returning backslider. To such languid and fainting, depressed and despairing, hesitating to return, doubting God's welcome, evidences lost, soulbeclouded, fears rising, hope veiled, the strongest cordials of God's most gracious, full, and free promises are needful to rouse, revive, and reassure the wanderer that the Lord invites, receives, and welcomes the returning backslider – the child retracing his way back to his forsaken Father.

God addresses them as backsliding *children*. He can never forget his parental relation to them, though they may forget or abuse their filial relation to him. Children though we are, adopted, sealed, and inalienably entitled to all the covenant blessings of adoption, we are yet backsliding children. The heart is ever swerving from God. The renewed soul possesses the principle of its own departure, contains the elements of its own declension, and but for the electing love, the restraining grace, the illimitable power of God, would destroy itself entirely and forever. Having in a former treatise[1] gone somewhat at length into the nature, causes, symptoms, and recovery of spiritual declension, my object now is specifically to meet that state of lukewarmness, tenderness, and hesitancy which marks the tremulousness of the contrite heart returning to God.

The language in which God addresses you is most reassuring. He calls you 'children'; though a backslider, yet a child. Can the human parent ever forget, in the deepest provocation of his offspring, that still he is his child? God here meets his wanderer just where that wanderer stands most in need of a divine assurance. What relation is it which spiritual backsliding the most contravenes, which sin the most obscures, and of which unbelief and Satan, presuming upon that backsliding, would suggest to the mind the strongest suspicion and doubt? We answer, the relation of divine sonship. The backslider reasons thus: 'Is my adoption real? Can I be a child of God, and prove so base, sin so deeply, and depart so far from my God? If a son, why am I so rebellious, disobedient, and unfaithful? Surely I cannot belong to the adoption of God and grieve and wound the Spirit of adoption thus?'

Now God meets the wanderer just at this critical juncture. He declares that though a backslider, yet he is still his child, and that no departure however distant

_____

[1] *Personal Declension and Revival of Religion in the Soul*, first published 1841. Banner of Truth 1993

and that no sin however aggravated, has impaired the strength or lessened the tenderness, tarnished or shaded the lustre of that relation. If God, then, comes forth, and, despite our backsliding, recognizes our sonship and acknowledges us as his children, who shall dispute or contravene the fact? 'Let God be true, but every man a liar' (*Rom.* 3:4).

Such, beloved, is the first consolation I suggest to your sad and depressed soul. Could it be surpassed by anything else I may offer? What, does God still call you his child? Does he not disown and disinherit you as a son of God and an heir of glory? Ah, no! He cannot forget that he has predestinated you to the adoption of children, that his Spirit has been sent into your heart, and that in happier days gone by you have often called him 'Abba, Father'. And although you have been rebellious, backsliding, and stiffnecked, yet, taking with you words and turning to the Lord your God, he meets you as once he met his repenting, mourning Ephraim, 'I have surely heard Ephraim bemoaning himself. Is Ephraim my dear son? is he a pleasant child? for since I spake against him, I do earnestly remember him still: therefore my bowels are troubled for him; I will surely have mercy upon him, saith the LORD' (*Jer.* 31:18, 20). Clear is it, then, that God's children do backslide; that it is no strange thing that their love to him should wax cold, their faith decline, their strength decay, their zeal slacken, their godly frames grow sleepy and inert, the spirit of prayer be restrained, the means of grace be neglected; and, as a consequence of all this inward declension, the world should have an ascendancy, Satan prevail, and the sin that does most easily beset them attain a momentary triumph. But still they are God's children –

oh wondrous grace! Oh changeless love! And, chastened, corrected, rebuked, and humbled, their heavenly
Father will restore them to his pardoning love and gracious favour, and they shall again walk with him filially,
humbly, softly, as his dear children, 'when I am pacified towards thee for all that thou hast done' (*Ezek.* 16:63).

What an invitation! 'Return!' It is God who speaks it,
the God from whom we have revolted, departed, and
gone so far astray. It is the word of our Father, against
whom we have rebelled, so deeply, so grievously sinned.
He shackles his invitation with no conditions. His simple
word is 'Return unto me!' And more than this, he has
placed before us an open door of return through Jesus
his beloved Son. The covenant of works provided no restoration for the soul that departed from God under the
first testament. But the covenant of grace has this distinction, this glorious feature: it places before the
penitent backslider, the contrite child, an open door of
return, a way of restored pardon, joy, and peace, and
bids him enter. The Lord Jesus is this open door. The
blood of Jesus, the righteousness of Jesus, the intercession of Jesus, the grace of Jesus, the quenchless love of
Jesus, the outstretched hand of Jesus, unite in guiding
the trembling footstep of the returning soul back to its
Father. The present efficacy and the continuous presen-
tation of the Lord's sacrifice in heaven, blended with his
intercessory work, personally and constantly prosecuted
before the throne, are a warrant that this door to God
shall never be closed while there lives a penitent sinner
to enter it.

Beware of shading the lustre of this truth – the present efficacy of the blood. The blood of Jesus Christ
'cleanseth' (*1 John* 1:7); it is in the form of the present

tense the great truth is put. The past is gone, the future all to us unknown, it is with the present we have to deal. A present sorrow needing comfort, a present perplexity needing guidance, a present burden demanding support, a present sin needing forgiveness, with a present Saviour prepared to meet and supply it all. Grasp this truth with all the intensity of your faith under present circumstances. Brood not over what is past, yield to no forebodings and fears as to what may be the future, grapple with the present. For in it you have a door which God himself has opened and which neither man, nor Satan, nor sin, shall shut. You have a throne of grace now inviting your approach; and you have the blood of Jesus with which to enter, as new, as efficacious, as prevalent, and as free as when it streamed from his sacred body on the cross. Let there be no postponement, then, of your return to God. Tarry for no more favourable moment, wait not for a better frame, dream not that Christ will be more willing to present, or that God will be more ready to receive you at any future time than now; or that by delaying you will be more worthy of his acceptance. Vain reasoning! God says, 'Return unto me', and he means by this, 'Return now!'

And what is the promise? 'I will heal your backslidings.' Backsliding from the Lord involves wounds, bruises, dislocation. It wounds the conscience, it bruises the soul, it breaks the bones of our strength and causes us to travel in pain and halting many a weary step. Ah, there is nothing so wounding as departure from God! Nothing so bruising of the soul's peace and joy and hope as sin! Who can heal, who can bind up, who can mollify, who can reset these broken bones so that they shall rejoice again, but our sin-pardoning God? We have no self-power in this great matter of restoration. All that *we* can do is to make burdens, forge chains, carve crosses, inflict wounds – in a word, destroy our own selves. Listen to David's experience: 'I have gone astray like a lost sheep.' This is all that he could do. But mark his conscious help-lessness, 'seek thy servant'; and then observe the imperishable nature of the grace of God in his soul, 'for I do not forget thy commandments' (*Psa.* 119:176).

Of how many who bend over these pages will this be a faithful portrait! Lord, I can leave thy fold, can wilfully depart from thy ways, can basely turn my back upon thyself; but thou must go in quest of me, seek and restore my soul; and this I may venture to ask, since I have not forgotten the happy days when thy candle shone upon my head, when thy light guided me through dark-ness, when the name of Jesus was as ointment poured forth, when I walked in sweet and holy communion with thee, and fed with the flock beside the Shepherd's tent. 'I do not forget thy commandments.' God will forgive! Christ will bind up the broken heart! The Comforter will restore joy to the soul! There is still balm in Gilead and a Physician there. The healing balsam still bleeds from the wounded, stricken Tree of Life. The gate of paradise is yet unclosed, its portal garlanded with a thousand exceeding great and precious promises, all inviting your entrance and insuring you a welcome to its sunny banks, its shaded bowers, its peaceful quiet streams. 'Who is a God like unto thee, that pardoneth iniquity, and passeth by the transgression of the remnant of his heritage? he retaineth not his anger forever, because he delighteth in mercy. He will turn again, he will have compassion upon us; he will subdue our iniqui-ties; and thou wilt cast all their sins into the depths of the sea' (*Mic.* 7:18–19).

What glad tidings these astounding words contain to repentant backsliders! What a bow of promise and of hope do they paint upon the dark cloud of despair which enshrouds the soul! 'He will turn again.' Though he has turned a thousand times before, yet, 'He will turn *again*'; not 'seven times' only, but 'seventy times seven'.

And what is the response of the returning soul? 'Behold, we come unto thee; for thou art the LORD our God.' Behold, we come just as we are! We come from the swine's trough; we come from feeding upon husks, upon ashes, and upon the wind. We come with the bruise, the wound, the dislocated limb. We come deploring our fall, confessing our departure, mourning over our sin; receive us graciously, love us freely, and turn thine anger away from us. 'I will arise and go to my father, and will say unto him, Father, I have sinned' (*Luke* 15:18). What after all that I have done, in the face of my wilful transgression, of my base ingratitude, of my abused mercies, of my past restorings, of my aggravated departures, of all the past of thy mercy, thy goodness, thy faithfulness, thy love, dost thou still bid me return? Does the overture, the outstretched hand, the first step, come from thee? Then, behold, I come unto thee, for thou art the Lord my God! Thy power draws, thy goodness dissolves, thy faithfulness binds my heart, and, lo I come! Thy grace restores, thy love pardons, thy blood heals my soul, and behold, I come. Thy voice, so kind, invites me; thy feet, so unwearied, seek me; thy hand, so gentle, leads me; thy look, so loving, so melting, so forgiving, wins me: and, Lord, I must not, I dare not, I cannot stay away. Behold, I come unto thee!

Jesus, let thy pitying eye
Call back a wandering sheep;

False to thee like Peter, I
  Would fain like Peter weep.
Let me be by grace restored;
  On me be all long-suffering shown;
Turn and look upon me, Lord,
  And break this heart of stone.

Look as when thy grace beheld
  The harlot in distress,
Dried her tears, her pardon seal'd,
  And bade her go in peace;
Foul, like her, and self-abhorr'd,
  I at thy feet for mercy groan;
Turn and look upon me, Lord,
  And break this heart of stone.

Look as when, condemn'd for them,
  Thou didst thy followers see;
Daughters of Jerusalem!
  Weep for yourselves, not me.
And am I by my God deplored,
  And shall I not myself bemoan?
Turn and look upon me, Lord,
  And break this heart of stone.

Look as when thy languid eye
  Was closed that we might live:
Father (at point to die
  My Saviour cried), 'Forgive';
Surely with that dying word,
  He turns, and looks, and cries, "Tis done!'
O my gracious, bleeding Lord,
  Thou break'st my heart of stone!

Thus have we sought to win back to Christ the strayed one and to help the returning wanderer heavenward. If the Lord has graciously given you to experience his restoring mercy, forget not one great reason why you are restored – that you might hate and forsake the cause of your departure. If we have succumbed to temptation, it is not enough that we have broken from its snare; if we have fallen into sin, it is not enough that we have escaped from its power. God would have you learn thereby one of your holiest lessons – the deeper knowledge of that which tempted and overcame you, that you might go and sin no more. Restored yourself, seek the restoration of others. Hear the injunction of Christ to Peter in view of this recovery, 'When thou art converted, strengthen thy brethren' (*Luke* 22:32). Seek to bring souls to Jesus. Let this be an object of life. Be especially tender, gentle, and kind to Christians who have fallen into sin and are thereby wounded, distressed, and despairing. Extend a helping hand to lead them back to Christ. Your deep abhorrence of the sin must not be allowed to lessen your compassion and sympathy for the sinning one. Jesus did not do so. If the church has vindicated her purity and allegiance to Christ by a wise and holy discipline of the offender, 'Sufficient to such a man is this punishment, which was inflicted of many. So that contrariwise ye ought rather to forgive him, and comfort him, lest perhaps such a one should be swallowed up with overmuch sorrow. Wherefore I beseech you that ye would confirm your love toward him' (2 *Cor.* 2:6–8).

Thus Paul charged the church to which he wrote, and in so doing he but imitates his Lord and Master, who, with a look of forgiving love, could comfort and restore his fallen apostle Peter. 'Be ye therefore followers of God, as dear children' (*Eph.* 5:1).

It is no uncommon thing for the Lord's backsliding children to be sadly and sorely distressed and cast down by certain portions of God's Word, containing delineations of character and denunciations of woe which they suppose applicable to themselves. So applied, these inconceivably aggravate their soul distress, their mental anguish, and incapacitate them from receiving the promises and accepting the comfort which God in his Word so profusely and so graciously extends to his children returning from their backslidings with weeping and mourning, confession and prayer.

Among the declarations thus referred to, which are supposed to have the most direct application and to wear the most threatening aspect, are those so frequently quoted and as frequently misinterpreted and misapplied, found in Hebrews 6:4–6:

> For it is impossible for those who were once enlightened, and have tasted of the heavenly gift, and were made partakers of the Holy Ghost, and have tasted the good word of God, and the powers of the world to come, if they shall fall away, to renew them again unto repentance; seeing they crucify to themselves the Son of God afresh, and put him to an open shame.

Such are the solemn words, often perused and pondered with terror and despair by the child of God, which we now propose briefly to consider and explain. But before venturing upon their exposition, let me from the outset distinctly and emphatically give it as my judgment that they in nowise refer to the case of the regenerate, and that by no ingenuity of criticism and by no perversion of error can they be made to bear strictly upon a state of real grace or to invalidate in the slightest degree the elect of God. Thus affirming our belief that the persons referred to by the apostle were not true converts to Christianity, had never passed into a state of spiritual regeneration, let us take each separate clause of these remarkable passages and endeavour, in the fear of God, rightly to explain and properly to apply his own truth.

'Those who were once enlightened' – not spiritually or savingly enlightened. The persons to whom these passages refer had some perception of the doctrines and principles of Christianity, the mind was intelligent, the judgment informed, but nothing more. They had received the knowledge of the truth in the intellect, but not the quickening, sanctifying power of the truth in the heart. It was an illumination of the mind only. As another wrote, they were so enlightened as to 'see the evil effects of sin, but not the evil that is in sin; to see the good things which come from Christ, but not the goodness that is in Christ; so as to reform externally, but not to be sanctified internally; to have knowledge of the gospel doctrinally, but not experimentally; yea, to have such light into it as to be able to preach it to others, and yet be destitute of the grace of God'.

This is the enlightenment of which the apostle speaks, and nothing more. Their religion would, in modern terms, be denominated the religion of the intellect, a religion which, however sound in its orthodoxy and logical in its reasoning, is but as a palace of ice floating amid the snows and gloom of the polar seas. But this description cannot apply to you, penitent child of God! The truth as it is in Jesus has enlightened your judgment and from thence has penetrated your heart, and in its light you see the sinfulness of your backslidings, the consciousness of which has brought you in sorrow and confession to the Saviour's feet. It is safe, therefore, to conclude that you are not one of those persons whom the apostle describes as being once enlightened, as having swerved from the truth, whom it was impossible again to recover, seeing they had rejected the evidence upon which they avowed their belief in and their attachment to Christianity, the only evidence Christianity offers in proof of its divinity.

'And have tasted of the heavenly gift.' A slight difference of opinion has existed as to the 'gift' here referred to; some expositors, among whom is Owen, make the next clause explanatory of the present one. Without, however, perplexing the reader with needless criticism, we at once offer it as our opinion that the 'heavenly gift' is the same as the 'unspeakable gift' referred to in another place and by the same writer. It is quite possible for an apostate from the truth, having the illumination we have spoken of, to have possessed a certain knowledge of Christ, 'the heavenly gift', without being renewed, sanctified, or saved. Does not Paul speak of his no more knowing Christ after the flesh (2 *Cor.* 5:16), as some still do, with a carnal, fleshly knowledge? Does he not, in another place, describe the conduct of some who had so far tasted of the heavenly gift as to 'preach Christ', but to preach him with envy, and strife, and contention, not sincerely (*Phil.* 1:15–16)? And yet again, is it not true that the same apostle warns certain individuals against the sin of eating the bread and drinking the cup of the Lord unworthily (1 *Cor.* 11:27)? What does all this prove but that those who have tasted of the heavenly gift have no other knowledge of Christ than that which is natural, notional, and speculative? They have not Christ in their affections, Christ as the object of supreme delight and love, nor Christ in them the hope of glory.

But you have not so learned Christ, O trembling penitent! It has pleased God to reveal his Son in you. You have tasted, felt, and handled, with a living, appropriating faith, the Lord Jesus. Your taste of this heavenly gift has been a heart-experience of his preciousness and fulness. And although you have gone astray like a lost sheep, yet you have not forgotten the power and savour of his precious name, which is now more than ever to you as ointment poured forth. And now your heart pines and your soul yearns to retrace its steps, to walk once more with the Shepherd whom you have forsaken, and to lie down again with the flock from whom you have strayed. What does this stirring within you prove – this contrition, self-abhorrence, and sin-loathing – but that you are not an apostate from the faith, a wanderer only from the fold, back to whose pasture and repose the faithful Shepherd is gently conducting you?

'And were made partakers of the Holy Ghost.' This clause is more clear and definite. How far an individual may be said to partake of the Holy Ghost and not be savingly converted has been long a debated question. These words, however, place the matter beyond doubt. The unhappy persons to whom they refer were undoubtedly partakers of the Holy Ghost, but in what sense? Let it be remembered that it was a distinctive feature of the early church that there existed within its pale those who were endowed, some with ordinary, and others with extraordinary gifts of the Holy Ghost; such as the power of working miracles, of prophesying, and of speaking with tongues, and that these persons were possessed of and exercised in many instances these gifts as instruments of pride, covetousness, and ambition – the works of the flesh in alliance with the gifts of the Spirit! Such, for example, was Simon Magus, who sought these supernatural endowments not for the glory of God, but as sources of gain, and as ministering to his carnal aspirations.

In his famous letter on 'charity', addressed to the church at Corinth, Paul recognizes the fact that he might be so far a partaker of the Holy Ghost as to speak with the tongues of men and of angels, and understand all prophecies, and all mysteries, and yet be destitute of the Holy Spirit's regenerating grace. And clearly it is to such individuals our Lord so pointedly and solemnly refers in his awful description of the judgment, when he says, 'Many will say to me in that day, Lord, Lord, have we not prophesied in thy name? and in thy name have cast out devils? and in thy name done many wonderful works?' (*Matt.* 7:22). To whom he will say, 'I never knew you: depart from me, ye that work iniquity' (*Matt.* 7:23). In the absence of the miraculous gifts of the Spirit, which we believe to have ceased in the church with the last of the apostles, men may still be endowed with many ordinary spiritual gifts, conferring upon them a name, placing them upon a pinnacle of the temple, and winning for them the admiration and homage of their fellows, who yet are destitute of the converting grace of the Spirit. This is all that is meant by having been 'made partakers of the Holy Ghost'. But your case, penitent believer, bears no analogy to this. What does your present contrition, your distress and anguish of soul prove, but that you are quickened with spiritual life and that the Holy Ghost dwells in you; that, despite your sinfulness, waywardness, and follies, the grieving and wounding and quenching he has received at your hands, the Spirit has not utterly departed from you, but that still your body is his temple and your heart his home?

'And have tasted the good word of God.' The meaning of this clause is obvious. The revealed Word, more especially the gospel of God, is the only interpretation it will

admit. These false professors, these wilful apostates of whom the apostle writes, had heard the Word of God with the outward ear, and had so far tasted its power as to yield an intellectual assent to its doctrines, and even to have felt some transient emotion, some stirring of the natural affections by the sublime and awful tenderness of its revelations. They had marked, too, the extraordinary power and triumph of the truth in the souls of others, and, moved by the law of sympathy, they were for a while the subjects of a natural and evanescent joy. They had witnessed the power of Satan in the human soul – how the gospel overcame it; the spell which the world wove around the heart – how the gospel had broken it; the period of perplexity – how the gospel had guided it; the season of sorrow – how the gospel had consoled it; the hour of sickness – how the gospel had strengthened it; the bed of death – how the gospel had smoothed it; the darkness of the sepulchre – how the gospel had illumined it; the fear of perdition – how the gospel had quelled it; the hope of salvation – how the gospel had confirmed it; the glory of immortality – how the gospel had unveiled it; and their hearts were thrilled with a transient glow of gladness. Such were the emotions of Herod when he sent for John, did many things, and heard him gladly. And such, too, was the case of the stony-ground hearers, who heard the Word, and anon received it with joy, but by and by they were offended, and fell away, not having root in themselves. These are they who had 'tasted the good word of God', and this is all that they had experienced of its power. But that is not your experience, sorrowing soul! You have more than tasted, you have eaten of the good Word of God, and his Word is unto you the joy and the rejoicing of your heart.

In that Word your longing, sorrowful soul now hopes –
upon it, weary and sad, your heart now rests until God
shall fulfill its promise and restore unto you the joy of his
salvation.

'*And the powers of the world to come.*' The age to come,
as the word has been, and we think properly, rendered.
Clearly the allusion is to the Messianic age, or the time
and dispensation of the Messiah. This was the age, or
the 'world to come', to which the apostle refers in another place: 'The world to come, whereof we speak'
(*Heb.* 2:5). He is clearly referring to the gospel, in contra-
distinction to the legal dispensation; in the latter the
word was spoken by angels, in the former the word was
spoken by Christ. This age, or gospel dispensation, was
to be ushered in and distinguished, 'both with signs and
wonders, and with divers miracles, and gifts of the Holy
Ghost' (*Heb.* 2:4). Now, it will not be difficult to trace the
application of this to the apostates whom these passages
describe. They had lived in the early dawn of the gospel
age and amidst its most wondrous and stirring scenes.
They had beheld these signs, had marked these wonders, and perchance had wrought these miracles. And so
they had 'tasted of the powers of the world to come'. All
this finds no application to your case, O backsliding yet
returning child of God!

Now follows the sentence of the Holy Ghost upon
these apostates from the profession of their faith. That
sentence is the most solemn, the most terrible, that ever
lighted upon the human soul. '*It is impossible....if they
shall fall away, to renew them again unto repentance; seeing
they crucify to themselves the Son of God afresh, and put him
to an open shame*' (*Heb.* 6:6). The key to the explanation of
this awful mystery is found in the word 'repentance'.

Could they become the subjects of true repentance there
might be hope, but with them this was impossible. For
the fearful sin which they had committed, no repentance was provided; for the deep guilt which they had
contracted, no sacrifice had been offered; from the apos-
tasy into which they had plunged, no avenue of return
had been made; in a word, for the crime with which
they were charged, no remission was given. Their salvation was impossible! After having professed to believe in
and to have received the Messiah as the Son of God, as
the Saviour of men, they had openly and wilfully and
utterly rejected him. By so doing they had repaired to
Gethsemane and justified the treacherous betrayal of
Christ by Judas; they had gone to Calvary and ratified the
cruel murder of Christ by the Jews; they had fraternized
with his enemies and had joined their shout, 'Away with
him! Away with him! Crucify him! Crucify him!' And so
they had 'crucified the Son of God afresh, and put him to
an open shame'. After having passed through all these
stages of sin, crime, and guilt, having utterly abjured and
renounced the only means and object and grace of repentance, it was impossible that they could be renewed,
recovered, and saved! For them 'there remaineth no
more sacrifice for sins, but a certain fearful looking for of
judgment and fiery indignation, which shall devour the
adversaries' (*Heb.* 10:26–27).

But, beloved child of God, we are persuaded better
things of you, and things that accompany salvation. The
Holy Ghost has given you the truest, the strongest evidence of spiritual life in your soul – a broken and a
contrite heart. Bring this sacrifice and lay it upon Christ
our Altar, and God will accept it. Let the holy lessons we
learn from the mournful, the irretrievable, the hopeless

case of the wilful apostate be: not to rest on spiritual illumination, however great, nor on spiritual gifts, however
eminent, nor on religious feelings, however ecstatic; but
seek after the mortification of sin, a closer communion
with the Lord, and still more to abound in those 'fruits of
righteousness, which are by Jesus Christ, unto the glory
and praise of God' (*Phil.* 1:11). Upon you these awful
words fling no darkling shadow, but your path is that of
'the just, [which] is as the shining light, that shineth
more and more unto the perfect day' (*Prov.* 4:18).

> *Welcome, weeping penitent;*
> *Grace has made thy heart relent:*
> *Welcome, long-estranged child;*
> *God in Christ is reconciled.*
>
> *Welcome to the cleansing fount,*
> *Springing from the sacred mount;*
> *Welcome to the feast divine,*
> *Bread of life, and living wine.*
>
> *Oh, the virtue of that price,*
> *That redeeming sacrifice!*
> *Come, ye bought, but not with gold,*
> *Welcome to the sacred fold.*

CHAPTER 10

The Swelling of Jordan

How wilt thou do in the swelling of Jordan?
— Jeremiah 12:5

We remarked in an earlier part of this work that the history of the children of Israel was strikingly illustrative, if not designedly typical, of God's spiritual Israel. And although, as in all illustrative and typological teaching of the Bible, we should bear in mind the marked ascendancy of the truth typified above the type, the thing symbolized above the symbol, yet there are always points of analogy and assimilation strictly true, impressively instructive, and strikingly beautiful, which it is our wisdom to study and apply. The emancipation of God's people from the iron furnace of Egypt, their march across the desert, their passage over Jordan, and their final settlement in the land of Canaan, are indisputable points of agreement and present at one glance the moral map of the Christian's pilgrimage and journey from earth to heaven. And yet, as we gaze upon the two pictures and contrast Pharaoh with Satan, the curse with Egypt, the wilderness with the heavenly pilgrimage, Jordan with death, Canaan with heaven, and Moses with Christ, we feel the force of the truth, how impotent is all material and earthly imagery to illustrate things spiritual and heavenly.

We select, however, from these interesting points of history one only as illustrating an important and solemn stage in the believer's journey – the passage of the children of Israel over Jordan. The church has for ages been wont to consider, and not improperly, this event as foreshadowing the Christian's departure to glory by death, while with it has been blended the most solemn, tender, and holy thoughts, feelings, and anticipations that ever found a house in the believer's heart. Approaching the end of this volume, we feel there would be lacking an essential link in the chain of helps heavenward were we to omit gathering around the closing scene of the believer's life those appropriate instructions, soothings, and hopes essential to the succouring of the soul in so solemn and momentous a stage of its history. Doubtless to the eye of the children of Israel, as they stood upon its banks surveying the promised land beyond it, the intervention of Jordan was an object of gloom and terror. And as its waters, dark and cold, rose and swelled, and broke in mournful cadence at their feet, as if in anticipation chanting the sad requiem of their death, we can easily imagine the question arising in many a sinking heart, 'How shall I do in the swelling of this Jordan?' Ah! how many who bend in sadness and trembling over these pages, to whose sick-chamber or dying-bed they will travel, are resolving in their anxious breasts the question, 'How shall I be able to meet death, how pass over this swelling flood, how may I meet this last, this latest, this most terrible crisis of my being?' Be still, these fears! Hush these doubts, child of God, while we endeavour to show how you shall fearlessly, safely, and triumphantly pass through the swelling of Jordan and reach your heavenly home at last.

'The swelling of Jordan' are words of solemn import, calculated to convey to the believing mind a gloomy idea of death. That there are swellings of Jordan in the Christian's experience we doubt not. For example, there are the fears with which the child of God anticipates the last enemy, there are the sad recollections of all his past sins crowding around his pillow, there are the suggestions of unbelief, perhaps more numerous and powerful at this moment than ever, and there is the shrinking of nature from the final wrench, the last conflict, the closing scene – the last glance of earth, the last look of love, the loosing of those fond and tender ties which entwine us so closely with those we leave – these are some of the swellings of Jordan. But oh, what are these in reality to the believer in Jesus? Nought but the gentle ripple on the surface!

Let me cite, as illustrating the groundlessness of your fears in anticipation of death, the history of the passage of the church in the wilderness over Jordan. We read that God commanded that twelve priests, representing the twelve tribes, should bear the ark of the Lord before the people, and that the moment the soles of the feet of the priests that bore the ark were dipped in the brim of the water, the waters rose up on either side; and then we read that 'the priests that bare the ark of the covenant of the LORD stood firm on dry ground in the midst of Jordan, and all the Israelites passed over on dry ground, until all the people were passed clean over Jordan' (*Josh.* 3:17).

Now here we have a beautiful representation of the passage of the children of God through death into heaven. Take each particular. There was present, first, the ark of the covenant. Borne upon the shoulders of the priest, it went before and led the march of the advancing hosts. That ark was a special and glorious type of the Lord Jesus. Christ, our divine Ark, has already clave the waters of Jordan, for he has passed through death in advance of his people. And still the Ark is with them. Never was the departure of a believer unattended by the presence of Jesus. Delightful thought! Christ our Ark will divide the dark waters as we pass, will go before, will go with us, will be our rearward, and thus encircled by Christ, amid the swelling of Jordan, we will fear no evil. What more is needed than the sensible presence of the Saviour to raise the heart superior to the fear of death, and to bear the soul tranquilly across the river? Fear not, then, believer, you will see his smile, you will hear his voice, you will feel his hand, and his conscious presence will enfold you as you pass.

Then, the feet of the priests stood firm in the midst of Jordan. The waters had parted, and on either side they stood as crystal walls of defence, while the hosts of the Lord passed over. Infinitely firmer do the feet of the saints stand on Christ when they die. The Rock on which you stand is a firm rock, the covenant of grace which you grasp is a sure covenant, the love of God in which you confide is an unchangeable love, the atoning work upon which you rest is a finished and accepted work. The throne of God in heaven stands not firmer than does the weakest and most fearful who, leaning on Jesus, clinging to Jesus, is sustained by Jesus, as he cleaves his way through the swelling of Jordan.

And then we are told that all the people passed clean over. What an impressive illustration of the full salvation of the whole Church of God! All the people – the small

as the great, the timid as the bold, the weak as the strong
– not one was left upon the shore, but all went over and
stood an unbroken column on the other side. Blessed
thought, the Church of Christ shall be finally and fully
saved, not one shall be left upon the bank, not one shall
perish amid the swelling of Jordan! You have often
mused, 'How shall I meet the final conflict? Will faith as
weak, will grace as little, will knowledge as limited, will
experience as shallow as mine be able to cross the swelling flood?' But why these fears? Why these misgivings?
Why these doubtful reasonings? Weak as may be your
faith, small your grace, limited your experience, you
shall not perish, for it is not your hold upon Christ, but
Christ's hold upon you, that insures your safe and certain passage over.

There are many other considerations well calculated
to disarm the believing mind of its fear of death, apart
from those we have stated. Let me briefly remind you of
a few.

Jordan was the passage to Canaan; death is the passage to heaven. Beyond the 'swelling flood' faith discerns
the better land, the fair haven, the glorious and eternal inheritance of the saints. Let this thought exert a soothing
influence on your mind. And then, to this add a kindred
reflection, that, on the other side of Jordan you will greet
again the loved ones from whom you parted on this side
of the river. Our home circles are thinning; vacant places
around our domestic hearth remind us that some, who
sat with us there, have passed over. Friend after friend is
departing, familiar and loved faces are disappearing from
our view, and life seems more lonely and the world more
desolate. Well, be it so. We shall find all who sleep in Jesus
again on the other side of the river. We accompanied

them to the banks of Jordan, saw them enter the swelling tide, heard their shout of victory, and then they vanished from our sight and we saw them no more. And soon our time will come, when we, too, shall pass over and meet them all again. A touching incident, which we venture to quote, illustrates this train of thought:

A father and mother were living with their two children on a desert island in the midst of the ocean, on which they had been shipwrecked. Roots and vegetables served them for food, a spring supplied them with water, and a cavern in the rock with a dwelling. Storm and tempest often raged fearfully on the island.

The children could not remember how they had reached the island; they knew nothing of the vast continent; bread, milk, fruit, and whatever other luxury is yielded there, were things unknown to them. There landed one day upon the island four Moors in a small boat. The parents felt great joy and hoped now to be rescued from their troubles; but the boat was too small to take them all over together to the adjoining land, so the father determined to risk the passage first.

Mother and children wept when he embarked in the boat with its frail planks and the four black men were about to take him away. But he said, 'Weep not! It is better yonder, and you will all follow soon.' When the little boat returned and took away the mother, the children wept still more. But she also said, 'Weep not! In the better land we shall all meet again.'

At last came the boat to take away the two children. They were frightened at the black men and shuddered at the fearful sea over which they had to pass. With fear and trembling they drew near the land. But how they rejoiced when their parents appeared upon the shore, offered them their hands, led them into the shade of lofty palm trees, and regaled upon the flowery turf with milk, honey, and delicious fruits. 'Oh, how groundless was our fear!' said the children; 'We ought not to have feared, but to have rejoiced when the black men came to take us away to the better land.'

'Dear children,' said their father, 'our voyage from the desert island to this beautiful country conveys to us a yet higher meaning. There is appointed for us all a still longer voyage to a much more beautiful country. The whole earth, on which we dwell, is like an island. The land here is, indeed, a noble one in our eyes, although only a faint shadow of heaven. The passage hither over the stormy sea is death; that little boat resembles the bier, upon which men in black apparel shall at some time carry us forth. But when that hour strikes, then we, myself, your mother, and you, must leave this world. So fear not. Death is, for pious men who have loved God and have done his will, nothing else but a voyage to the better land.'

Be not over anxious as to the time, the place, or the mode of your passage over Jordan. As death is in the covenant, so are all the circumstances of death likewise in the covenant, and they will transpire just as your covenant God has fixed and arranged. Ah, how many feel the swelling of Jordan more in groundless, anticipative fears than in actual reality! Be not anxious, beloved, about this matter. All is in the Lord's hands, and he will divide the swelling billows and take you dryshod over, and not a heaving, not an undulation of the cold waters, shall chill the warmth or ruffle the calmness of your breast.

> Where *shall I die? Shall death's cold hand*
>   *Arrest my breath, while dear ones stand*
> *In silent, watchful love, to shed*
>   *Their tears around my quiet bed?*

Or shall I meet my final doom
    Far from my country and my home?
Lord, to thy will I bend the knee,
    Thou evermore hast cared for me.

How shall I die? Shall death's stern yoke
    Subdue me by a single stroke?
Or shall my fainting frame sustain
    The tedious languishing of pain?
Sinking in weariness away,
    Slowly and sadly, day by day?
Lord, I repose my cares on thee
    Thou evermore hast cared for me.

When shall I die? Shall death's stern call
    Soon come my spirit to appall?
Or shall I live through circling years
    A pilgrim in this vale of tears,
Surveying those I loved the best,
    Who in the peaceful churchyard rest?
Lord, I await thy wise decree;
    Thou evermore hast cared for me.

My unconverted reader! how will *you* do in the swelling of Jordan? Momentous question! All of us must die. The wicked and the righteous, the godly and the ungodly, the friend and the foe of God, all, all must bow to this law of our nature, this sentence of our humanity. Have you seriously pondered this question, 'How will it be with me in death?' You are living now a Christless, a prayerless, a godless, a hopeless life. You are living in sin, for self, and with no reference whatever to the solemn hour you are to meet, the awful event you are to confront, the fearful account you are to surrender: after death, the judgment (*Heb.* 9:27). With no real preparation for death, how do you think you will meet the judgment? As death leaves you, judgment finds you. The awful scrutiny transpires, the tremendous account is demanded the moment that your unclothed spirit is hurried hence. The instant that your probation ceases, your final and changeless destiny begins. What will, what must be the end of your present persistent course of irreligion? You are living as if you were a god to yourself, as though God your Creator furnished you with those intellectual endowments, gave you those talents, lavished upon you those advantages, that wealth, influence, and rank only to gratify your own ambition, promote your own selfish ends, and to minister to your perverted taste, carnal, earth-bound aspirations and desires. But no! God created you for a higher life, for a nobler end, for a more glorious being, for a sublimer destiny. He created you – your person, your mind, your gifts, your social position, your wealth – in a word, your body, soul, and spirit, your present and your future, for himself.

Man, woman, I tell you, God created you for his own glory, and he will not fail of that one and sublime end of your creation, whether it be secured by his vengeance or his grace, by his justice or his mercy, by lifting you to heaven or sinking you to hell. I revert to the momentous question: What will you do when the dark, cold waters of death are swelling and surging and deepening around you? What will your rank avail you? What will your wealth do for you? What will your talents profit you? What will your pleasures supply at that moment when the curtain is falling upon all the false shadows of time and is rising upon all the dread realities of eternity? But there is yet hope! Fall in penitence at the Saviour's feet and grasp in faith the Saviour's sacrifice, and you are saved! Then

Jordan will have no dread swellings for you, death no sting, the grave no gloom, eternity no terror.

Pharisee! What will *you* do in the swelling of Jordan? When your self-righteousness fails to support you, when your Babel of good works is crumbling around you, when your foundation of sand is sliding from beneath you, and the religion you have cherished is leaving you without support, without comfort, without peace, without hope, what then will you do? Death is confronting you! You have entered the river. It is dark, cold, and heaving; it deepens, surges, moans; it floats you from the shore of time; it bears you on to the ocean of eternity, and you disappear – a soul lost, *lost* forever! Oh, cast from you the garment of your own righteousness, and accept in faith the Saviour's, and then death's waters will waft you upon their gentle swelling safe to glory, and you shall be a soul saved, *saved* forever!

Anxious, sin-burdened soul, how will you do in the swelling of Jordan? Will you take with you those convictions, that load of guilt, to the brink of the river? Oh no, part with them now and forever! Lay them down at the cross, cast them at Jesus' feet, and in faith plunge in the sea of his atoning blood, and you need not dread the river of death.

Dying saint, look at death through Jesus, and how lovely will it appear! Christ invests every object beheld by faith through him with beauty and attraction. Oh, thou shalt fall in love with death, and be enamoured of the grave, if thou wilt view them both through thy dying, risen, living Lord! It is not with death you have to do, it is with death's Conqueror. Descend, then, to the river with a firm, unfaltering step,

Shudder not to cross the stream,
Venture all thy hopes on him;
Not one object of his care
Ever suffer'd shipwreck there.

I put the question to the sincere, humble believer in Jesus: How will *you* do in the swelling of Jordan? You reply, 'I will cleave closer and closer to Jesus. As the waters deepen, I will plant my foot of faith firmer and firmer upon the Rock, until I find myself in glory.' Then, fear not the swelling tide! Death will be to you – looking to Jesus, clinging to Jesus, accepted in Jesus – but a falling asleep, a translation from the family of God on earth to the family of God in heaven, a going from the church below to the church above. It is but a narrow stream that divides you, as seen by faith. You may go down to the margin of the river, weeping and lamenting as you go:

Oh! could I make my doubts remove,
These gloomy doubts that rise,
And see the Canaan that I love
With unbeclouded eyes!

Could I but climb where Moses stood,
And view the landscape o'er,
Not Jordan's streams, nor death's cold flood,
Should fright me from the shore.

But when you enter, your tears will cease to flow, and your song will commence, and your departure shall be like that of Bunyan's pilgrim, 'Valiant for the Truth', which that master of allegory thus inimitably describes:

'My sword I give to him that shall succeed me in my pilgrimage, and my courage and skill to him that can get it. My marks and scars I carry with me, to be a witness for me that I have fought his battles who will

now be my Rewarder.' And when the day that he must
go hence was come, many accompanied him to the
river-side, into which, as he went, he said, 'Death, where
is thy sting?' and as he went down deeper, he said,
'Grave, where is thy victory?' So he passed over, and all
the trumpets sounded for him on the other side.

> Whither can a sinner flee?
>   Who, oh who, will rescue me?
> Dreading my deserved sentence,
>   Weeping tears of deep repentance!
> Yawning grave! I fear to die,
>   Such burdens on my conscience lie!
>
> Hark! I hear my Saviour say,
>   'I can take thy guilt away;
> I have bled that men might live,
>   Full salvation I can give:
> I will help thee, soul distress'd,
>   Come unto me – I'll give thee rest!'
>
> Almighty Lord! I know thy voice,
>   In thee believing I rejoice,
> My Prophet, Priest, and King!
>   Now I can sing of joys on high,
> 'O grave, where is thy victory?
>   O death, where is thy sting?'

CHAPTER 11

Our Father's House

My Father's house.
—John 14:2

Our adorable Lord came down to earth to allure us up to heaven. In all his delineations of that happy, holy place, he sought to present it to the believing eye clad in its richest beauty and invested with its sweetest and most winning attractions. Its hope was to sanctify us, its prospect was to animate us, and its foretastes were to comfort us. Nothing, therefore, was wanting in the imagery with which he pictured its character and in the colouring with which he painted its glory to invite and attract us to its peaceful, blissful coasts.

It may, indeed, be said that Christ's allusions to heaven were not frequent and that his revelations of its state were but partial. Be it so. Sufficient, however, of the veil was uplifted to reveal the fact of its existence, to awaken the desire and to inspire the hope of its possession. We cite, as illustrating this, the words at the head of this chapter. They are few, but how expressive! Heaven is portrayed as our Father's house. What a precious, endearing, attractive view does this give us of our future and final rest, our eternal abode! 'My Father's house!'

How touching the words! How many hallowed associations, sunny memories, and precious thoughts cluster around the image! If there is one earthly spot dearer, sweeter, brighter than another, it is the home of our childhood. Around it, when years and oceans and continents have long and far severed us from its hearth, our fondest, warmest thoughts and recollections still cling. And we think, when sickness and loneliness and want steal upon us, could we but return to that home again, and again feel the warm embrace of a mother's love, and find ourselves beneath a father's sheltering roof, life would be a pleasant thing. Thus Christ portrays our heaven. He tells us it is a house, a Father's dwelling, and that within its walls there are many mansions, one of which awaits each of us; and then, he bids us not to be troubled in heart by reason of the sorrow and privation of our present exile, since before long he will come and take us home.

The fatherhood of God is the first truth our Lord propounds in connection with this picture of heaven. It was a natural and befitting introduction to his attractive theme. In speaking of the Father's house, he would first reveal to us the parental relation of God. We could never have given to this truth the grasp of faith it demands had not Christ revealed and explained it. It was he who first taught our lips to say, 'Our Father!' In asserting his own relation as an Elder Brother, he flung around the entire brotherhood the filial bond that linked both himself and them to the same God and Father. Oh, how dimly and imperfectly we realize to what dignity and privilege and glory a sinner's union with the Lord Jesus exalts him! It is a relation to God but one remove from his own. Who would not be willing to forego all the righteousness of man, all the purity of saints, all the holiness of angels, to stand in the righteousness of the Lord Jesus Christ? Now, it must be acknowledged that in asserting the fatherhood of God in reference to himself, our Lord adopted, as the 'first-born among many brethren', the most effectual mode of instructing us in a knowledge of the same filial relation. In claiming God as his Father, he claimed him as ours too. How beautifully and touchingly were the traits of that filial relation exhibited in his own personal spirit and demeanour! Each act of his brief but eventful life was imprinted with filial confidence and love, and his whole career was a continuous recognition of the Fatherhood of God. Let us cite a few examples.

Do we speak of prayer? Hear him cry, 'O righteous Father, the world hath not known thee: but I have known thee' (*John* 17:25). 'I knew,' Father, 'that thou hearest me always' (*John* 11:42). Do we speak of duty? Hear him exclaim, 'Wist ye not that I must be about my Father's business' (*Luke* 2:49)? Do we speak of reverence? Hear him say, 'Even so, Father: for so it seemed good in thy sight' (*Matt.* 11:26). Do we speak of submission? Listen to his words, 'Not my will,' O my Father, 'but thine, be done' (*Luke* 22:42). Do we approach the solemn scene of his death? Hear him exclaim amidst the maddening tortures of the cross, the thunders of God's anger, the lightning of God's justice rolling and flashing above and around him, 'Father, into thy hands I commend my spirit' (*Luke* 23:46). Do we track his footsteps to the mount from the summit of which he went back to glory? Hear his parting words, 'I ascend unto my Father, and your Father' (*John* 20:17). And as we return from these hallowed scenes, we ask ourselves: Is it any marvel that he, the Elder Brother, who could so embosom himself in the Fatherhood of God, should teach our faltering lips when we prostrate ourselves before the divine Majesty of heaven and earth, to breathe the prayer, 'Our Father which art in heaven' (*Matt.* 6:9). O beloved, allow your heart no repose and the Holy Spirit no rest until he seal Abba, Father, upon your heart! It would be impossible to compute or exaggerate the results that would follow from the blessing. What a mighty impetus would it give you heavenward! With what new-born power would it clothe your prayers! What soothing would it impart in suffering, what submission in trial, what sweetness to obedience! With what increased beauty and charm would it invest the whole landscape of life, its checkered scenes of joy and sorrow, sunshine and shade, and in what a glow of golden light would it bathe the distant vision of the Father's unseen home to which Christ is conducting you! See, the heavenly Dove flutters over you, waiting to descend, as upon the baptized Son of God, testifying to your divine sonship, turning your darkness into light, your sorrow into joy, your distrust into confidence, your fears into hope, and the condemnation you dread into a heaven assured! 'Behold, what manner of love the Father hath bestowed upon us, that we should be called the sons of God' (*1 John* 3:1). We turn our attention now from the Father to the Father's house.

We have alluded to the hallowed attractions and the sunny memories which cluster around the paternal home. Transfer your thoughts, my reader, from the earthly to the heavenly – take the purest, the fondest, the most poetic conception you can form of the one, and blend it with the other – and still you have but the faintest analogy of heaven! And yet you have made some approximation to the idea. You have entwined around your heart the image and hope of heaven as your home. Earth has some foreshadowings of this truth. If now we are the children of God, then ours is not a state of dreary orphanage; we are not fatherless and homeless. Christ reminded his disciples of this. 'I will not leave you comfortless' (*John* 14:18 – margin, 'Orphans'). If then, we are not fatherless, there is a sense in which we are not homeless – the lower rooms, the outer courts, the vestibules of the heavenly home, are found on earth, in which we meet and hold communion with our heavenly Father. What is the sanctuary, filled with his glory, the closet, hallowed with his presence, the chamber of sickness, soothed with his love, the hill-side, where at eventide we go to meditate, sanctified with his fellowship, but our Father's home coming down out of heaven to dwell a while with his children on earth? Where my Father is, there is my Father's house.

It may be remarked of many of the ungodly that they go through a hell to hell; with equal truth it may be affirmed of the children of God, that they pass through a heaven to heaven. Our Father's house is a house of 'many mansions', and earth is one of them. The universe is his abode, every sun and star his dwelling-place; why should we exclude him from this our own planet, though one of the smallest, yet, in its history, the greatest, the grandest of all? The whole family on earth and in heaven claim him as the one Father, and earth and heaven are but parts of the one home. And oh, if earth – the vestibule, the portico of heaven – is so radiant with glory, what must be heaven itself!

> *Since o'er thy footstool, here below,*
> *Such radiant gems are strewn,*

Oh, what magnificence must glow,
    My God, about thy throne!
So brilliant here those drops of light,
    There the full ocean rolls – how bright!

If night's blue curtain of the sky,
    With thousand stars inwrought,
Hung like a royal canopy,
    With glittering diamonds fraught,
Be, Lord, thy temple's outer veil,
    What splendour at the shrine must dwell!

The dazzling sun, at noontide hour,
    Forth from his flaming vase,
Flinging o'er earth the golden shower
    Till vale and mountain blaze,
But shews, O Lord, one beam of thine;
    What, then, the day where thou dost shine!

Ah, how shall these dim eyes endure
    That noon of living rays,
Or how my spirit, so impure,
    Upon thy glory gaze!
Anoint, O Lord, anoint my sight,
    And robe me for that world of light.

While, therefore, we would not exclude earth as one
of the mansions of the Father's abode, seeing it is the
temporary dwelling-place of so great a portion of the
family, we must still view it as but one of the lower rooms,
hallowed and radiant indeed with the Father's presence,
yet by service and discipline designed but to prepare us
for the state-rooms above, the higher and nobler mansions to which before long we shall be summoned. Now,
let us transfer our thoughts to the Father's house above
and endeavour to portray its spiritual architecture and its
domestic privileges, not trespassing upon the region of

the fanciful and ideal, but keeping soberly and strictly within the teaching of God's Word.

'In my Father's house there are many mansions' (*John* 14:2). Guided by these words, the first view which it presents to the mind is its appointed and prepared state. We go to no uncertain home. It is the family mansion, eternally ordained and prepared for the dwelling of the saints. The everlasting love which chose us to salvation, the predestination which appointed us to be sons, provided the home we were eternally to occupy. What a sweet truth, beloved, is this! Do we not, when after a long exile we turn our face homewards, delight to think that we shall find our home all ready for our welcome? Such is our heavenly abode. 'For we know that if our earthly house of this tabernacle were dissolved, we have a building of God, an house not made with hands, eternal in the heavens' (2 *Cor.* 5:1). The apostle, too, reminds us that it is 'an inheritance incorruptible, and undefiled, and that fadeth not away, reserved in heaven for you' (*1 Pet.* 1:4). And did not our blessed Lord declare the same truth when He said, 'I go to prepare a place for you' (*John* 14:2)? We go, then, to a home all appointed and prepared, all garnished and made ready for our coming. And oh, if, with regard to an earthly home,

> *'Tis sweet to think there is an eye will watch*
> *Our coming, and look brighter when we come,*

infinitely more delightful is the thought that not one alone, but many eyes are now looking and watching for our coming to glory and will gleam with deeper lustre when we come! Ah yes, we shall find all prepared, anticipating our arrival, when we reach that blessed abode! It is even now ready: the crown glitters, the palm waves, the white robe flutters, and the harp is all strung and tuned by Christ's own hands. This suggests another thought.

The solemn hour of death once passed, the spirit, upborne by angels, finds itself at once ushered into the reception-room of heaven, the first of the 'many mansions'. There we shall see Jesus not seated but standing, as when he rose to receive his first martyr, to welcome us home, encircled by the general assembly and church of the firstborn, the spirits of just men made perfect, and an innumerable company of angels waiting to greet our arrival. In advance, and more eager than all the rest of that blessed throng, will be the loved ones from whom we parted on the banks of the river across which they passed to the Celestial City. Oh, what a reception, what greetings, what wishings of joy then! 'Welcome, husband! Welcome, wife! Welcome, child! Welcome, parent, brother, sister, pastor, friend!' will burst from ten thousand times ten thousand lips, louder than the voice of many waters.

But the Saviour's welcome will be the crowning one of all! With what ineffable joy will he receive home the fruit of his long and weary travail, the sheep that often wandered from his side, and had as often been restored, but now will wander no more! The disciple that often wounded the bosom that sheltered him, had as often been forgiven, but now will wound it no more! Oh, who can imagine the infinite joy of that Saviour when the celestial convoy ushers into his presence the sinner he ransomed by his blood, called by his grace, kept by his power, and in spite of all, through all, and out of all, at last brought home to his Father's house? Blessed Lord, not one, the purchase of thine agony – not a sheep straying from thy fold, not a lamb sheltering in its weakness at thy side, not a sinner, stricken, wounded, raising its penitent and believing eye to thy cross – shall be wanting then to complete the number of thine elect, the roll-call of thy redeemed Church. All, all shall be there! 'Thou shalt guide me with thy counsel, and afterward receive me to glory' (*Psa.* 73:24).

The heavenly repast, which succeeds the reception, will introduce us into the banquet hall of heaven, another mansion of the Father's house. We have remarked that there are bright gleams of heaven falling upon earth's shadows. Among the most resplendent of these are the foretastes of the banquet which awaits us on high. The Church of Christ thus joyously records her experience of this truth: 'He brought me to the banqueting house, and his banner over me was love' (*Song of Sol.* 2:4). What a chord in your heart do these words touch, O believer! It was Jesus who brought you! By the drawings of his love, the leadings of his sovereign grace, having sought and found, separated and called you, he led you gently and persuasively to his church, richly stored with all blessings, where he made you to sit in heavenly places. He brought you, too, in a stately manner, his all-conquering standard floating above you, upon which his name of Love was inscribed. Oh, admire and glorify the grace that brought you into this house of wine, to banquet with the King, and forget not that whatever may be the Lord's dealings with you, that all-shielding and overshadowing banner of love still floats above you!

The gospel banquet is another foretaste of the heavenly. It is thus described by the evangelical Isaiah: 'In this mountain shall the LORD of hosts make unto all people a feast of fat things, a feast of wines on the lees, of fat things full of marrow, of wines on the lees well refined'

(*Isa.* 25:6). How full and rich is the gospel of Christ! How divine the provision, how ample the supply, how free the invitation! The forgiveness of all and every sin, your reconciliation with the offended Majesty of heaven, peace so divine, so great in your soul that it 'passeth all understanding', life and immortality, the consummation and crown of its blessings! Oh, pray for and cherish a spiritual zest for this banquet! Bring to it your soul's craving, your spirit's weariness, your heart's sadness, your sin-woundings, your worst and lowest frames; there is enough in its unfoldings of Jesus to satiate every weary soul and to replenish every sorrowful soul. There Christ will nourish you with the finest of the wheat; with honey from the rock will he satisfy you. Never forget that such is the fulness of the gospel of Christ, such its variety of blessings, such the sufficiency of its supply, and such the freeness of its bestowment, that it meets every case, every trial, every phase, and every lack of our humanity! What a banquet, too, is the Lord's Supper, where, perhaps, the brightest gleams of glory fall, since that, of all other institutions of Christ, the most closely unites and blends the atoning death, and the millennial glory of Christ. 'As often as ye eat this bread, and drink this cup, ye do show the Lord's death till he come' (*1 Cor.* 11:26). How strangely, yet appropriately, are the cross and the crown of Jesus entwined in this sacred festival! Both are associated with our sweetest exercise of faith, hope, and love. Faith, with undimmed and steady eye, looks at the cross; hope, with expanded and untiring wing, soars onward to the crown; and love prostrates itself before both in adoring gratitude and praise.

Such are some of the foretastes; let us now consider the heavenly banquet itself. Our Lord thus distinctly and emphatically refers to it: 'I appoint unto you a kingdom, as my Father hath appointed unto me; that ye may eat and drink at my table in my kingdom' (*Luke* 22:29–30). And in a gospel parable he yet more graphically portrays the festival in the narrative of a certain king who prepared a sumptuous banquet in honour of his son and sent forth his servants to invite them that were ready. It is on this occasion the memorable scene of the intruder without the wedding garment is introduced. The door of the banquet hall is thrown open, and the king arrayed in royal apparel, with ineffable delight beaming in his countenance, enters the chamber all resplendent with the purest light and redolent of sweetest odours to survey and welcome the guests. It is at this moment the discovery is made of the stranger; and the man who refused the appropriate garment provided by the king and presumed to enter attired in his own is expostulated with, sentenced, and removed from the scene of splendour and festivity into outer and eternal darkness! The great and momentous truth our Lord sought to illustrate and enforce is, my reader, essentially connected with your future and endless well-being, namely, the absolute, indispensable necessity of being invested with the imputed righteousness of Christ as giving us a title and a fitness for the heavenly banquet. Without the wedding garment you cannot appear with acceptance at the wedding supper. Without the investiture of Christ's justifying righteousness – your own utterly, entirely, unreservedly, and forever abjured, renounced, and forsaken – you appear at the banquet hall of glory only to confront and sustain a doom all the more confounding, overwhelming, and dire than the presumptuous hope you had vainly cherished. Oh, it is a fearful plunge as from the very door of heaven into the abyss of hell; as from the streaming light of glory into the outer darkness of the bottomless pit! Oh, come away from your doings and your failings, from your merit and demerit, from the things you have done and the things you have not done, from the keeping of religious days and fasts and festivals, from all the fond conceits of goodness, holiness, and righteousness in yourself, from all self-approval, self-justification, self-trusting, and as a sinner betake yourself to the righteousness of Christ, accept it as a free gift, put it on in faith; and from that moment you shall be found complete in Christ, and robed for the banquet of heaven.

Of the banquet we know but little. Our blessed Lord was studiously partial and reserved in his revelations of heaven. It would seem as if he would deepen our surprise and enhance our joy by the present concealment he carefully observed. And yet he has told us sufficient and revealed enough to intensify our panting to be there. This much we know, that heaven is not a state, but a place; not boundless space, but a locality; not the dwelling of a host where we shall sojourn a while as guests, but our Father's house, where we shall be children at home forever. We are assured, too, that its nature, its employments and pleasures, will, in all respects, be genial to the condition and will comport with the capacity, dignity, and immortality of our unclothed and glorified nature. The soul, divested of all that is material and gross, will be fitted to enter into all that is spiritual and pure. The banquet that your redeeming God will have prepared for you will accord with the nature he had fitted for the banquet. And, oh, what imagination can adequately conceive the costliness, the richness, the variety, the ever-augmenting material of that heavenly repast with which the glorified will regale themselves through eternity? How will the mind revel amid the ever-unfolding wonders of God's mind! How will the heart feast upon the ever-unfolding depths of Christ's heart! How will the soul dilate and repose in its ever-deepening, ever-growing happiness! Dim as our views of heaven are, surely it were enough to satisfy our most intense aspirations – the assurance that we shall be perfectly holy. Advance me to a condition of sinlessness, to a place where holiness sanctifies every heart, beams in every eye, breathes from every lip, sparkles in every action, of which every thought, and word, and look, and act, is its expression and embodiment, and you have placed me at the richest banquet God can provide or my heart desire. 'In thy presence is fulness of joy; at thy right hand there are pleasures for evermore' (*Psa.* 16:11). Lord, number us among the blessed who shall eat bread in thy kingdom, and who shall be called unto the marriage-supper of the Lamb, at thine appearing and glory.

The Father's house has also its music-mansion. Adoration and praise would seem to constitute the principal employment of the redeemed in heaven. The visions of glory which floated before the eye of John were all associated with music. To his sea-girt isle were wafted the strains of the song sung by the hundred and forty and four thousand who stood on Mount Zion. In his lonely exile he heard the harpers harping with their harps. And of whom was that celestial choir composed? The 're-deemed from among men' (*Rev.* 14:4). And who and what are the subjects of their song? Jesus and his redemption. 'Thou art worthy...for thou wast slain, and hast redeemed us to God by thy blood out of every kindred, and tongue, and people, and nation' (*Rev.* 5:9). Blended with the song of redemption will be the song of providence. Retracing all the way thy God led thee through the wilderness, thou shalt gather material from each mercy and from each trial, from each joy and from each sorrow, for an eternal hymn of praise to his great and glorious name. Beloved, you are learning these songs now in the house of your pilgrimage. As you cross the desert sands, or break your lone footsteps through the depth of the wilderness, or stand within the sacred shadow of the cross, God is preparing you for the music-mansion of glory. All his dealings with you in providence and in grace are but to train and attune the powers, affections, and sympathies of your soul to the sweet harmony of the spheres. Every sunbeam of mercy that gilds your path, and every cloud-veil of judgment that shades it, every heavy footstep of the giant storm, every gentle wavelet dimpling the calm surface of the soul, every soft zephyr that lulls it to repose, is designed by God to instruct and mature you for the music of the celestial state. A harp of gold strung by angels and attuned by Christ's own hands awaits you in the music-mansion above, and soon you will sweep its chords to the high praises of the triune Jehovah and all heaven will ring with its melody.

> *Arise, my soul, arise,*
>   *Unfold thy heaven-born wings;*
> *Thy home is in the skies,*
>   *Where lofty Gabriel sings;*
> *And loud, through all the spacious plain,*
>   *Is heard – 'The Lamb, the Lamb was slain!'*
>
> *Oh, may my bosom glow*
>   *With melody like this!*

Oh, may my spirit bow,
  When musing on their bliss!
Ah! didst thou die, dear Lamb, for me?
  He bled – he groan'd – he died for thee.

Oh, teach me that new song
  Which occupies their time;
And say, will it be long
  Ere I shall reach that clime?
I'll wait till thou shalt call me home;
  Yet come, Lord Jesus, quickly come.

Is there a harp for me?
  (Oh, gently chide my fears!)
Is there a throne for me
  Beyond the rolling spheres,
Where joys unchanging ceaseless flow,
  And sin or death shall no one know?

The throne-room of heaven is not one of the least appropriate and gorgeous mansions of the Father's house. The saints of God are a kingdom of priests, a royal priesthood, the heirs of a kingdom. And no character in their glorified state will be more visible and distinct than their regal one. The expectation of an earthly kingdom – the dream of the early Christians – our Lord dispelled by announcing that his kingdom was not of this world. But while he thus sought to inculcate more spiritual views of the nature of his church, he at the same time broadly declared the fact of their present royalty and of their future reign. 'And Jesus said unto them, Verily I say unto you, That ye which have followed me, in the regeneration when the Son of man shall sit in the throne of his glory, ye also shall sit upon twelve thrones, judging the twelve tribes of Israel' (*Matt.* 19:28). The apocalyptic vision of the seer confirmed this statement. 'And I saw thrones, and they sat upon them; . . . and they lived and reigned with Christ' (*Rev.* 20:4). Our glorified Lord again referred to the enthronement of the saints in his cheering words addressed to the Christian combatant: 'To him that over-cometh will I grant to sit with me in my throne, even as I also overcame, and am set down with my Father in his throne' (*Rev.* 3:21). 'Be thou faithful unto death, and I will give thee a crown of life' (*Rev.* 2:10). Such, believer, are your royal and resplendent expectations. A public and glorious enthronement and coronation awaits you. A royal priest, you will before long be made like Christ, a 'priest upon his throne' (*Zech.* 6:13). Emerging from your present 'incognito' – the ignorance of the world and the cold neglect of the church – you will be ushered into the throne-room of glory, saints and angels will escort you to your seat, and amidst the hallelujah chorus of countless myriads, Christ will crown you a king and a priest unto God, and you shall reign with Jesus forever and ever. Oh, whatever obscurity may now veil your relation as belong-ing to the royal seed, let your demeanour be such as to stamp you with the character once ascribed to Gideon's brethren, of whom it was said, that 'each one resembled the children of a king' (*Judg.* 8:18).

We are trespassing not upon the region of imagina-tion when, in depicting the spiritual architecture and appointments of the Father's house, we refer to the picture-gallery as constituting one of its most appropri-ate and attractive mansions. It is not materializing heaven to transfer to its spiritual descriptions the expres-sive imagery of the material. In so doing we but imitate the Holy Ghost, who, in all his spiritual delineations of glory, hesitates not to dip his divine pencil in the bright, gorgeous colours with which God has tinted and enamelled this beautiful world.

Painting as a historic art is universally and practically acknowledged. As the handmaid to history, her aid and achievements have won the gratitude and admiration of ages. Transfer the illustration to heaven. Upon the walls of that magnificent gallery, depicted in colours of living light, will be seen all the marvellous events of God's moral and providential government in the history of the universe, separately, visibly, and eternally traced. Nor this only. What will be our astonishment and marvel when we gaze upon the walls of that gallery to behold our individual history from our entrance into this world of woe to our entrance into the world of glory, each event, each epoch, each step delineated with a life-like truthfulness, a depth of tint, and a transparency of colour which shall reveal all the past with startling vividness, overpowering the mind with wonder, and expanding the heart with praise! Incidents which we had failed to note, events which we had totally forgotten, providences which we had blindly seen, and circumstances which we had strangely misunderstood, will then form a series of pictures, presenting a complete and perfect history of our individual life, illustrating the infinite wisdom, goodness, faithfulness, and love of our Father throughout the whole.

It is recorded of Queen Elizabeth that, ignorant of the laws of painting, she commanded her portrait to be taken without a shadow upon the canvas. With an ignorance of the laws of moral painting equally as profound and infinitely more serious, how often would we have obliterated from our history those sombre pencillings of life's picture – the dark background and blended shadows –

which the divine artist knew to be essential to the fidelity, harmony, and perfection of the whole! We would have life without its moral discipline. We would efface from the portrait all the shadings of sorrow and sickness, suffering, poverty, and bereavement, leaving nothing but the bright and sunny hues of unmingled, unclouded happiness. But when we wander through the interminable picture-gallery of our Father's house and gaze upon the carvings, the paintings, and frescoes of our whole life, each epoch, event, and incident – the highlights and shadows beautifully and exquisitely blended, looking down upon us with startling fidelity from its jasper walls – we shall then see the infinite rectitude of our heavenly Father in all his present dealings with us, both of sorrow and of joy. With what vividness shall we then see the necessity, as much for the cold, dark pencillings, as for the warm, roseate tints of the picture; and for both the lights and shadows, the joys and sorrows of life, we shall laud and adore his great and glorious name!

Among the many mansions there will not be wanting one which will especially recognize heaven as a place of study. What a library of knowledge, therefore, awaits us in our Father's house! Heaven is a place of thought, of expanded intellect, of matured and ever-enlarging and enriching mind. Our minds are but in the infancy of their being; and the themes of reflection and subjects of research which they grasp are necessarily graduated to our present infantile and limited powers. What an infinite sea of knowledge, upon whose shores we now but stand, is reserved for our higher life in glory! The library of heaven! How vast! How rich! What volumes for study will be the histories of the universe, of our world, of man, of redemption, of our individual life!

What exalted and sublime themes of thought, the being and character of God; the love, grace, and glory of Christ; the work, power, and gentleness of the Holy Ghost! In a word, what volumes for our study and research will be the book of providence and the book of grace! And will *The* Book have no place in that library? Verily, I believe that it will. I do not think that in the archives of heaven, the sacred scroll of God's revealed truth will be missing. That most marvellous of all wonderful books, the Bible – the parent, and source, and foundation of all that was accurate in history, true in philosophy, profound in science, rich in poetry, sound in ethics, and real in religion – will then unclasp its lids and unfold its leaves; and in a light that will explain every truth, elucidate every mystery, harmonize every discrepancy, we shall read the Bible as we never studied its wondrous contents before. Not a truth will be lost. It is recorded of a late historian that, had every copy of *Paradise Lost* been destroyed, such was the marvellous tenacity of his memory, he would have been able to have reproduced every sentence of that poem. Is it too much to affirm that, so engraved, engrafted, and inlaid is the precious Word of God in the souls of the regenerate, when every material copy of the Bible shall, with all that is merely human, have passed away, each truth of that divine revelation shall be reproduced, read, studied, and preserved forever in the library of our Father's house?

The subject which this chapter has but imperfectly discussed is most consolatory and sanctifying. Is it not a soothing reflection, that all those who depart this life in the faith of Christ we shall find again in the house of the one family? When we met their last look of love and caught their last words of blessing, and then laid their dust to rest until the trumpet of the archangel sound, we were ready to ask, 'Shall we see them again?' Oh yes, the gospel of Christ illumines the believer's grave with a living hope! On our arrival in the Father's house, we shall find them all again, not one absent who on earth possessed the firstfruits of the Spirit.

How productive is this truth of Christian union and brotherly love in the Church of God! In cultivating home feelings, domestic affections, and sympathies, in our anticipation of heaven, we shall instinctively feel drawn by a bond of irresistible attraction towards all who evidence their relation to the family of God. We shall prove our filial relation to God by our fraternal affection for his people. 'Every one that loveth him that begat loveth him also that is begotten of him' (1 John 5:1). Have we not all one Father? Are we not all brethren? Do we not sit at one table? And are we not all journeying to the same home? Why should we then fall out by the way? Why allow differences of judgment, or denominational distinctions, or party heats, suspicion, envy, and jealousy – those wretched fruits of the flesh – to sunder and alienate us the one from the other? Must not a lack of love like this be grieving to the heart and dishonouring to the name of our one Father? Let us no longer speak of tolerating a child of God, or deem it condescension to fraternize with one of the Lord's saints because he belongs to another branch of God's family. Away with such spurious Christianity! Rather let us, in the meek and loving spirit of the Elder Brother, feel ourselves honoured in ministering to him in the lowliest office of Christian service, everywhere and on all occasions recognizing and loving him as a brother beloved of God, and thus recognize, love, and honour the Father in his child. Oh for more Christ-like love in the family of God! This I consider to be the great, the chief need in the professing Church of Christ in the present day. I speak not of differences of judgment, or modes of worship, or of denominational branches; these have existed, do exist, and will exist until Christ comes to unite all his people in one body, and blend all in one worship, and behold the answer to his prayer and the consummation of his desire: 'That they all may be one' (*John* 17:21). But I speak of a lamentable deficiency of that love which may and should exist despite ecclesiastical position, which derives not its inspiration, form, and tint from a denominational source or mold, but which proceeds pure and holy from God, and in its influence on the church binds and assimilates in oneness of spirit, in fellowship of heart, and in unity of service all who are the children of God by faith in Christ Jesus.

Let us aim to model and to mould our earthly homes after the heavenly. There righteousness dwells, holiness sanctifies, love reigns, perfect confidence and sympathy and concord exist. Why should not the earthly homes of the righteous be types of this? The domestic constitution is a most marvellous and benevolent appointment of God and is designed, among other ends, to unite, strengthen, and sanctify the different relations of life and thus secure and promote the mutual happiness and well-being of each and all. Thus God would make the family relation a type of his church on earth and in heaven. But, alas, how has sin perverted this! What place of misery are some homes on earth, even where religion is supposed to have found a temple and a shrine! Discord, where there should be harmony; suspicion, where there should be confidence; jealousy, where there should be delight; coldness, distance, and alienation, where there should be the warmest, closest, and most endearing intercourse; harsh, abrupt expressions, where there should be nought but pleasant words, the profoundest interest and sympathy – in a word, hatred, where there should be love. But, beloved in the Lord, this should not be so with you! And with you it is an individual matter, for our homes are just what the individual members of the family make them. One unhappy temper, one unbending will, one unloving, unsympathizing heart may becloud and embitter the sunniest, sweetest home on earth. Oh, cultivate the affections, the sympathies, and the intercourse you hope to perpetuate in heaven! By mutual forbearance, gentleness, confidence, and love; by offices of kindness, delicate attention, and gracious demeanour, seek to transfer as much of the purity, love, and sunshine of your Father's house above as you can to your Father's house below. And then, when you ascend from the earthly to the heavenly, it will be but the transfer of home affection, intercourse, and happiness, cherished, cultivated, and sanctified here, to a higher and nobler sphere holy as God, enduring as eternity.

Let us cherish domestic thoughts and anticipations of heaven. This will make us long to be there. How confirmatory of this the dying testimony of some! Listen to their glowing language. 'Almost well, and nearly at home,' said the dying Baxter, when asked by a friend how he was. A martyr, when approaching the stake, being questioned as to how he felt, answered, 'Never better; for now I know that I am almost at home.' Then, looking over the meadows between him and the place where he was to be immediately burned, he said, 'Only two more stiles to get over, and I am at my Father's house.' 'Dying,' said the Rev. S. Medely, 'is sweet work, sweet work; home! home!' Another on his death-bed said, 'I am going home as fast as I can, and I bless God that I have a good home to go to'. What sweet and powerful attraction it has to quicken our pulse and to speed us onward to its blessed abode! Heaven is to some richer in love than earth. With many there are no relatives so close, no friends so dear, no hearts so loving, no minds so congenial as those in heaven. And still it grows richer! Earth's ties are loosening, life's relations are lessening, sacred friendships are narrowing, the purple clouds of our pilgrimage are disappearing, and soon we ourselves will be the last shadow that shall melt into eternity! But these holy ties, these hallowed relations, these sacred friendships, these heaven-enkindled loves, will all be found again in our Father's house.

> *World, farewell! my soul is weary;*
>   *I would here no longer stay,*
> *In thy desert wild and dreary;*
>   *Heavenward will I wend my way.*
> *World! in thee is war and strife,*
>   *Pride and vanity are rife,*
> *But in heaven there ever is*
>   *Peace and rest, and perfect bliss.*
>
> *On that blessed shore arriving,*
>   *Pain and sadness at an end,*
> *Done all anxious care and striving,*
>   *Resting with my dearest Friend!*
> *In the world is need and woe,*
>   *And at last death's bitter throe;*
> *But in heaven above shall be*
>   *Peace, and joy, and purity.*

What are earthly joy and pleasure?
  Cloud and mist and empty wind.
What are worldly wealth and treasure?
  Burdens for the weary mind.
World! in thee is war and strife,
  Pride and vanity are rife;
But in heaven is perfect peace,
  Rest, and all-enduring bliss.

Oh, what glorious songs are pealing
  From that chosen, spotless throng;
O'er the plains of heaven stealing,
  Holy, holy, still their song!
World! in thee are scoffs and jeers,
  Hatred, woe, and bitter tears;
While in heaven there ever is
  Peace, and rest, and perfect bliss.

Here is weeping and repining,
  Earthly joy not long endures;
If a while the sun is shining,
  Soon dark night his beams obscures.
World! deep anguish is in thee,
  And the final agony;
But in heaven above there is
  Peace, and rest, and perfect bliss.

There my Lord unveils his glory,
  I shall see him face to face,
And repeat the wondrous story
  Of a sinner saved by grace.
When the woes of earth are past,
  And death's bitter pang at last,
Then in heaven above will be
  Peace, and joy, and purity.

Oh to join the thrilling voices
Of that happy, sainted choir!
Each in Jesus Christ rejoices,
All their thoughts to him aspire.
In the world is war and strife,
Pride and vanity are rife;
But in heaven will ever be
Peace, and rest, and purity.

Cheer, my soul, the time is nearing
Thou thy Saviour's face shalt see;
Lovest thou thy Lord's appearing?
Joyful shall that moment be.
World! thou hast but storm and strife,
Fear and sadness, death in life;
While in heaven there ever is
Peace, and rest, and perfect bliss.

Now, in love without dissembling,
Saviour, school my willing heart,
That when worlds are round me trembling,
'Come,' I hear, and not, 'Depart.'
World! in thee is fear and care,
Sin and sadness everywhere;
But at home there ever is
Peace, and rest, and perfect bliss.

Father, I will that they also, whom thou hast given me, be with me where I am; that they may behold my glory (*John* 17:24).

Other Octavius Winslow *titles from
the Banner of Truth Trust:*

NO CONDEMNATION IN CHRIST JESUS

ISBN 0 85151 592 4

406 pp. Paperback

A verse-by-verse exposition of Romans 8, beginning with the promise of 'no condemnation' in verse 1 and moving to the assurance in the final verse that there will be 'no separation' from the love of God in Christ for those who belong to him.

PERSONAL DECLENSION AND
REVIVAL OF RELIGION IN THE SOUL

ISBN 0 85151 261 5

203 pp. Paperback

Winslow powerfully applies the themes of scriptural teaching in such a way that the reader is alternately humbled before the majesty of God and the cross of Christ, and lifted up by the love, mercy and grace of the Saviour. He reminds us that 'there exists not a day that every believer stands not in need of the restorings of the Lord'.

THE WORK OF THE HOLY SPIRIT

ISBN 0 85151 152 X

223 pp. Paperback

A classic on the work of the Holy Spirit in the life of a believer, originally published in 1840. Winslow demonstrates from Scripture that, 'All that we spiritually know of ourselves, of God, of Jesus and His Word . . . all the real light, sanctification, strength and comfort we are made to possess on our way to glory, we must ascribe to the Holy Spirit.'

For free illustrated catalogue please write to
THE BANNER OF TRUTH TRUST
3 Murrayfield Road, Edinburgh EH12 6EL, UK
P O Box 621, Carlisle, Pennsylvania 17013, USA